# AN INTRODUCTION TO

# CHURCH HISTORY

## *A BOOK FOR BEGINNERS*

BY THE

## REV. PETER GUILDAY, Ph.D.

*Secretary, American Catholic Historical Association*
*Professor of Church History, Catholic University of America*

Nam ut de Ecclesia primo loco dicam, quid ad laudem
ejus illustrius, quid ad defensionem fortius, quid ad
propagationem utilius; quid ad morum ac disciplinæ gravi-
tatem restituendam aptius proferri potest quam historia
rerum Ecclesiasticarum? Jamvero ad convincendos haere-
ticos nihil, meo quidem judicio, efficacius est atque poten-
tius quam hoc genus scriptionis.
Valesius, in preface to his edition of Eusebius (1695).

*SECOND IMPRESSION*

## B. HERDER BOOK CO.
### 17 SOUTH BROADWAY, ST. LOUIS, MO.
AND
### 33 QUEEN SQUARE, LONDON, W. C. 1.
1925

THE VAIL-BALLOU PRESS
BINGHAMTON AND NEW YORK

TO THE

MEMORY

OF

ALFRED CAUCHIE

Who died at Rome, February 10, 1922

## PREFACE

In compiling these pages out of that special library of books on historical method which every teacher of history gradually gathers to his shelves, the author's purpose was to prepare an outline for the use of beginners in the field.

A course of lectures to graduate students covering the historical method in its application to Church history cannot be given in less than three academic years—the usual time allotted for the preparation towards the doctorate. Time is lost at the opening of each academic year with those students who have entered the course for the first time. To second and third year students these lectures contain a twice-told tale.

In order to avoid repetition it was suggested that an outline be prepared, containing these initial lectures, and that the neophytes be permitted to use them privately so that they would be able to begin the more detailed work of historical criticism with the others.

When the suggestion was made to put this compilation into print, it was made on the score that the book would be welcomed in circles, especially in certain circles of the Catholic clergy, that seek a means of orientating themselves in so fascinating a study as that of Church history.

The writer yields to the suggestion with much misgiving. The chief drawback of such a volume is that it contains hardly more than a glimpse into what might be given on the subject.

Sincere thanks are due to the Very Reverend Francis P. Siegfried, Professor of Philosophy, at the Seminary of St. Charles Borromeo, Overbrook, Pennsylvania, for many corrections and suggestions in preparing the manuscript for the printer. The writer is specially indebted to Dr. Arthur Preuss of St. Louis, the editor of the *Pohle-Preuss Dogmatic Series* and of the *Koch-Preuss Handbook of Moral Theology* for his revision of the proofs of this volume.

*March 25, 1925*      PETER GUILDAY

# CONTENTS

# AN INTRODUCTION TO CHURCH HISTORY

## CHAPTER I

### THE MEANING OF CHURCH HISTORY

Among the many problems of perennial interest to the historian are those concerning the definition, the interpretation, the division, the aims and value, the science and the art of history itself. Despite the large number of books in many languages on these problems, agreement on them among historians is apparently as distant as ever. There are as many definitions of history as there are interpretations or philosophies back of these definitions. To a large extent the viewpoint of the historian will be found embodied in his formula for the essential factors of history. To an even larger extent these viewpoints have affected the periodization of the past. The question of aims and value, so all-important to the science of history since it determines the selection of the source material and its interpretation, is more open to argument at the present moment than at any time during the past half-century.

Where history ceases to be an art and begins to be a science, where it passes the border between literature and scholarly criticism of the source material upon which the artistic narrative is based, is a vaguely known fork in the road of its triumphal progress across the kingdom of knowledge. Yet, to be uncertain about any or about all of these problems must of necessity cloud the scientific character of history itself. To admit at the outset that only confused and confusing answers may be given to all these initial questions in historical development tells against the right of history to be considered as one of the major modern sciences. To try to answer these questions is very similar to allowing one's barque to swing out into mid-current without oars or rudder.

Nothing is more insecure in the present state of philosophic thought than to take for granted scientific definitions and distinctions, however old and widely accepted. Erasmus is credited with the remark that every definition is a misfortune. In the science of history definition has been piled upon definition until at present the tendency is not to choose any one out of the heap but to avoid the heap altogether. No commonly accepted definition of history exists. Frederick

Harrison strives to reach such a definition by clarifying the use of history and leaves the problem unsolved in a volume entitled *The Meaning of History*. Henry Johnson in one of the best books on the teaching of history ever written meets the question: What is history? with the generous answer: History is everything that ever happened.

History has a hundred different uses, we are told, and each particular use has given rise to its own particular definition. "In its amplest meaning," writes James Harvey Robinson in *The New History*, "history includes every trace and vestige of everything that man has done or thought since first he appeared on earth." Nothing is therefore nugatory in the survey of that historical past. The very vastness of that past makes History a vague term at the best and hence difficult to define with all the clarity and precision the true scholar must desiderate.

The student whose mental processes have been formed in the cold and rather unemotional school of Catholic philosophy is at a disadvantage in the presence of vague definitions of any sort. In discussing scientific problems with thinkers who are suspicious of rigid definitions from which all emotion has been wrung, he gradually realizes that the philosophy he possesses has never shown more caution than in the creation of scientific formulas. The old scholastics, his ancestors in the art of thinking, invariably began with a definition of the *word*. When this was clear, there followed a definition of the *thing*. The verbal or nominal definition, based upon the etymology of the word or upon its common or arbitrary use, was tempered to steel-like firmness by a real definition, explaining the thing itself:—either by its causes, its essential elements, its properties or accidents, by its genetic content or by its end or purpose.

The medieval scholastics went a step farther. They laid down rules for definitions; they distinguished between things that could be defined and those that might only be more or less accurately described. One has but to weigh in the balance-scales the essential meaning and the popular conception of such frequent terms as Inquisition, Infallibility, Reformation, Protestantism, Tolerance, Indulgences, Temporal Power, and Middle Ages, to realize the difficulty the scholar has in reaching a mutual understanding with the unlearned on these historical factors of the past.

It helps but little in approaching a clear, adequate, positive definition of history to inquire into the meaning of the word itself. The two senses in which the word *history* has been used—either the record of past events or the events themselves

—convey a double meaning which cannot be uni-
fied. "It is unfortunate," writes Professor Shotwell, "that such a double meaning of the word
should have grown up, for it is productive of not
a little confusion of thought." This confusion
blends from the nominal into the real definition;
and Johnson in his *Teaching of History* cuts the
Gordian knot of the problem by stating: "History admits of no very exact definition." Nevertheless scholars have defined it and will continue
to define it. Matthew Arnold in his *Lectures on
Modern History* defines history as the essence of
innumerable biographies, or the biography of a
political society or commonwealth. Hinsdale's
thought-provoking book *How to Study and Teach
History* contains a more accurate definition:
"In the broadest sense, history is the story of man
living in social relations in the world as traced
in various records and memorials; more narrowly, it is the story of man living in the higher
social relations that constitute the civil state or
civilization." Other definitions are well known:
—History is past politics; politics is present history. History is humanity becoming conscious
concerning itself. History is "a narrative told
of ourselves, the record of a life which is our
own, of efforts not yet abandoned to repose, of
problems that still entangle the feet and vex the
hearts of men." History is the narrative of

man's onward and upward march, upward from the brute and onward to the final goal of the human spirit in an effort to obtain eternal freedom in the possession of God. History is a voice forever sounding across the centuries the laws of right and wrong. History is a school that teaches what things in life are useful and to be followed and what things are injurious and to be avoided. History is a divine epic, and the historian a prophet, with his eyes turned backward. History is the science of the development of reason, and so forth.

These are some of the definitions still current in works of history. They are all well-known and their authors equally so. They do not exhaust the list. None of them helps us to reach the very heart of what history is. Must we admit with Flint that "to attempt further to define it would be worse than useless because it would be unduly to limit, and to distort and pervert, its meaning"? One factor can be admitted as essential to the definition of history: history is dynamic, not static. It is life, and it cannot be studied as a lifeless thing or walled off from life. Benedetto Croce in his *Theory and History of Historiography* has stated that every true history is contemporary history.

History must be defined, therefore, in terms of life. What life is, what its real aim is or should be, how life should be viewed——these are questions that are receiving confused answers in our day. In its viewpoint of life the modern world is in sharp contrast——the contrast of conflicting explanations——to the past. Whatever else the Middle Ages failed to do, they furnished every one from the child to the king with an answer to the *whence, why, whither* of life's philosophy. The historical investigations of the nineteenth century have thrown "such a painfully bright light" upon the contradictions in the newer philosophies regarding life, that one can only despair of ever reaching the true meaning of history in the present concept of life.

If we appeal then to scholastic philosophy to lead us out of the labyrinth of all these unsatisfactory definitions of history, we must expect to find ourselves in the land where the strict mental discipline of doctrinal explanation stands as a guide-post to all the factors involved in history. Time, space, nature, spirit, mind, soul, free will, God and the end of life——these have no uncertain meaning for a philosophy that saw its greatest master in Thomas of Aquino. Behind that philosophy stands the science to which it must ever be ancillary——theology. Both have the same source, and that source is divine. There can be no discord between them, for anything taught contrary to revealed truth is an abuse of philosophy, and things that are philosophically certain can not be contrary to those which are theologically certain.    Philosophy is independent of theology in this that it has for its object those things which are knowable by the light of reason; but it remains forever dependent upon theology as to a higher law, directing and correcting, if necessary, its conclusions.

This premiss excludes the entire question of the meaning of history from the modern court of interpretation.    To bring in the theological, or more narrowly, the eschatological, teaching of the Catholic Church, is derided at once as aprioristic.    The truth seems to be that every other interpretation of history is permissible except the Christian interpretation.    History has as its subject-matter man and the story of man's life on earth.    That man has been placed on the earth by the Creator for the very definite purpose of earning his salvation and of preparing himself for the life to come in the Beatific Vision of God is a truth that will never be accepted by those who follow any one of the various interpretations of history in vogue today.    What is the weakness of the theological interpretation of history? asks Professor Shotwell in his *Introduction*.    "It is," he says, "of the same character as that we have seen in the myth.    The interpretation is outside of history altogether." If we take his explanation of this viewpoint, it will be easy to understand the issue between the Catholic key to the world's progress and all others offered to the searcher for a complete and adequate interpretation of man's past.

History is still, to the Catholic, "the realization of religion—not of various religions, but of one; the working out of one divine plan." It is still "a vast, supernatural process, more God's than man's." It has still but one interpretation—the supernatural. Between this belief and the various theories proposed for the interpretation of the facts of history, there is at present no *via media*. The Catholic concept of history does not exclude the economic, the sociological, the idealistic, or the political theories of historical interpretation. It may, if it wishes, embrace them all, on condition that what is frankly materialistic in their processes be eliminated. But no one of these interpretations will accept the full measure of the Catholic concept of history or of civilization, on the basis of its irrelevancy to the field of history itself.

The new synthetic history, largely dominated by the latest trend of sociology to make itself a meeting-ground of all the sciences but giving form and design to none, attempts to see in the human mind and in its development the unifying thread in history. History thus becomes "the sum total of human achievements"; and in this guise the religious factor is given a place, and a prominent place, be it admitted, in the synthesis.

It is here that the roads fork. Religion cannot be accepted as merely one of many institutional factors in life. Religion—and by this word must be meant faith in Jesus Christ and His Holy Church—must dominate all these factors. God is the only Absolute. Man was created for the absolute happiness of God's presence. All else is relative, secondary, ephemeral, earthly.

The importance of this antinomy between Catholic and non-Catholic thought lies in its far-reaching effects. Definitions and divisions of history, the discussion of its aims and value, the processes of its scientific development—all are colored by the interpretation that lies hidden behind them. Thus W. P. Ker, in his *Philosophy of History,* can say: "There is an implicit philosophy of history in every modern historian, even when he may seem for the time to have no interest beyond the narrative." On the one hand there is sure footing; on the other, there is not only the fear of quicksands, but the treacherous quicksands themselves. On the one hand there is the sense of direction, the surety of the goal, the location of the harbor; on the other, there is a vagueness of the course, a half-mystical location of the port, an unknown destination. "The ships of non-Catholic thought are ever veering from one direction to the opposite, and thus make little headway. Now, for instance, they are engulfed by the quicksands of materialism, now they dash against the cliffs of idealism, now they lie becalmed in the land-locked bays of individualism, now again they are aground in the shallows of socialism. Meanwhile, the barque of Peter, guided by the pole-star of divine revelation, steers right on through mid-ocean, unswerving from the true course."

When, therefore, the Catholic definition of history is given, it is given in the light of the theological concept of man. To take at random one of the many definitions by Catholic historians will explain this dependence. "History," writes Alzog, "may be said to be a record of the development of mankind under the providential guidance of God; or more precisely, a record of the systematic training and improvement of the human race by divinely appointed means as a preparation for the birth of Christ, that God might, through the coming of His Son, secure from man a spontaneous homage and a worship worthy of Himself. The coming of Christ, in this view, gives a definite character to history, and the periods both before and after that event constitute its two grand divisions. This idea of history will be more striking and impressive, the more clearly it is understood that the human mind, enlightened, elevated, and purified, is alone able fully to comprehend the divine agency which was at work shaping the destinies of men both before and after the coming of Christ."

Such a definition will never be fully accepted, even by so-called Christian students of the processes of history, since it is based upon the doctrine that the whole philosophy of life is summed up in the statement that man is a creature of God, composed of body and soul, made in His image, and given the boon of life here on earth for the purpose of knowing Him, loving Him, and so serving Him in this world that he may be eternally happy with God in the world to come. And yet, to refuse to recognize the spirituality of the soul, its immortality, and the divine revelation given to ensure its destiny at the end of life's journey, is equivalent to a rejection of all definition of history.

Consequently, each and every definition of history offered as a solution of this first problem in the science—its meaning—must be analyzed in the light of its conformity to logic, weighed in the balance of its harmony with the fundamental Christian concept of life, and accepted or rejected on its merits as explanatory of the relative and ultimate ends of life. There is no harmony possible between the Catholic concept of life and the modern mechanistic concept, from which the economic, sociological, and materialistic interpretations of history are evolved. It is fair, just and equitable to halt on the threshold of the temple of history every pilgrim who comes without supernatural vision to view the beauties and the uglinesses, the joys and the sorrows, the comedies and the tragedies of the Palace Beautiful.

This does not mean, however, that the Catholic historian has the right to exclude all other factors but the supernatural in his own explanation of the past of humanity. All that he asks—all that he can and must ask—is that the religious factor in the fashioning of man and in man's destiny through the ages be understood and accepted as the dominant cause in the philosophy of history. Nor can he accept Professor Shotwell's ironic diagnosis of the confusion that reigns among the non-Catholic theories of history: namely, that all interpretations are relative; that in each age, from the mythological interpretation of the pre-Christian ages to the theological concept of Augustine, the medieval historians, and Bossuet, to the philosophical or deistic and the materialistic or economic interpretations of the past three centuries, there has been a series of progressive clarifications of the meaning of history.

There are today seven principal schools of interpretation for the explanation of the main causative factors in history: the theory of great personalities—*la théorie des grandes hommes,* the "drum and trumpet" history; *la théorie des grandes batailles,* the most noted exponent of which is the author of *Heroes and Hero-Worship;* the economic or materialistic explanation, systematized by Feuerbach and Karl Marx and their numerous followers, a cautious study of which will be found in Seligman's *Economic Interpretation of History;* the mechanistic or environmental theory, based upon the geographical factors, which owes much of its value to the studies of Montesquieu (*Esprit des Lois*), Buckle (*History of Civilization in England*), Semple (*Influence of Geographic Environment*), and to those of Ritter, Ratzel, and Ellsworth Huntington; the idealist, spiritual, or neo-Hegelian, which was found a warm advocate in Professor Shailer Mathew's *The Spiritual Interpretation of History,* but which must not be confounded with the supernatural interpretation of man's life on earth; the theory of natural science, which marks the stages of man's advance by the milestones of the evolution of the history of science; the sociological interpretation of history—to which such eminent names as Vico, Condorcet, Comte, and Spencer may be accredited, and which accounts for historical causation by a synthetic view of "the origin, growth, structure and activities of society through the operation of their physical, vital, psychological causes, working together in a process of evolution"; and the newer or synthetic, or the "collective psychological" interpretation of history, which today is in the leadership of thought in American historical circles, and of which a fairly clear exposition will be found in James Harvey Robinson's *New History*. Professor Robinson describes it as follows: "The 'New History' is escaping from the limitations formerly imposed upon a study of the past. It will come in time consciously to meet our daily needs; it will avail itself of all those discoveries that are being made about mankind by anthropologists and sociologists, discoveries which during the last fifty years have served to revolutionize our ideals of the origin, progress and prospects of our race. . . . History must not be regarded as a stationary subject which can only progress by refining its methods and accumulating, criticizing and assimilating new material, but it is bound to alter its ideals and aims with the general progress of society and the social sciences, and it will ultimately play an infinitely more important rôle in our intellectual life than it has hitherto done."

A clear exponent of the newer history, Professor Harry Elmer Barnes, defines its purpose in this wise: "The newer history refuses to look upon any phase of human conduct as unworthy of consideration, but it seeks to put due emphasis upon those classes of activities and interests which the slightest reflection upon human life must demonstrate always to have been the most vital and influential in human existence and development, namely, economic activities, social relations, technology and natural science, and political, legal and religious institutions."

Who shall say that in the honest, sincere, and impartial study of the past of humanity from this broad angle of vision, the religious factor in life will not gradually come back to its ancient place as queen of the dominating and motivating causes in the historical retrospect?

Great names in philosophy, in the historical sciences, and in scholarship are attached to all these schools of historical interpretation. It would not be accurate to state that the religious factor in the history of the human race is ignored completely—how could it be ignored?— by all these interpreters of the past. What they do wish to ignore, to exclude even, is the

eschatological view of life.  In this they have
succeeded, and probably no one factor is more provocative of proof than this—that for almost
three hundred years the Catholic historical interpretation of history has remained as Bossuet
left it in the seventeenth century.  It must be
remembered also that no one of these interpreters
honestly claims to have solved the riddle of
the universe.  All that we have at the present is
their vigorous exposition of past history, their
conscious shortcomings, and their eager desire to
reach the ultimate.  The sum total of all the discussion is hardly more than "an interpretation of
interpretations" and that in itself is a confession
of failure.

The newer synthetic history is already old.
It has had a rapid vogue and undoubtedly owing
to its very unity of viewpoint it deserves the
widest experimentation.  Unfortunately it is
still too young to have effected a revolution in
the second problem which constantly annoys the
historical student—the divisions of history.
Nothing cries so loud for change as the stereo-
typed periodization of history.  None of the interpretations listed above is responsible for the
unfortunate division of history into Ancient,
Medieval, and Modern.  They come to us from
Christoph Keller, who inaugurated them in his
compendiums about the end of the seventeenth

century. The three divisions belonged before that time to the science of philology. It is true that they are serviceable in splitting up a big subject like history, but they are so artificial that they have become misleading. It is here that the newer synthetic history may prove a blessing in disguise, since it may so completely revolutionize our views on the subject-matter of history, that all divisions will merge into the study of world history. Until that time comes, we shall no doubt continue to speak of Ancient, Medieval, Modern and Contemporary History, and continue to suffer under the mental confusion these terms connote.

Meanwhile, the student should understand the factitious nature of this classic division. There is no settled viewpoint on the *termini a quo* and the *termini ad quem* of any of these three or four divisions. Certainly, with the progress made in the science of man (anthropology), in the science of the mind (psychology), in the science of life (biology), in the science of industrial relations (economics), in the science of environment (anthropogeography), in the science of social relations (sociology), in the science of government (politics), and in the science of pre-literary history (archeology)—certainly with all this advance before us, the beginning of history must be pushed back many leagues beyond the conventional birth of historical knowledge. To close the so-called Ancient Period at any of the arbitrarily chosen political milestones, such as 313 (recognition of Christianity by Constantine), 378 (battle of Adrianople), 395 (division of the Empire into East and West), 476 (so-called fall of the Western Empire), 565 (the death of Justinian), 622 (the Hegira), 732 (the battle of Tours), or 800 (the coronation of Charlemagne)—to stop short at any one of these dates can only be the veriest makeshift for understanding the historical development of civilization. To close the Middle Ages with the end of the Crusades (1274), with the death of Dante (1321), the capture of Constantinople by the Turks (1453), the end of the Hundred Years War (1453), the expulsion of the Moors from Spain (1492), the discovery of America (1492), the voyage of Vasco da Gama (1498), or the rebellion of Martin Luther (1517)—is to admit the necessity of confusion in understanding one of the greatest ages of human endeavor. To close the Modern Period with the rise of the Metternich policies in 1815 is but to continue the political divisions which crowd the history manuals; and to begin Contemporary History with the French Revolution in 1789 is totally to misunderstand the "vast social reform in which the Terror was an incident."

The function of the date in history is merely "to keep an event in position while it is being examined and its relations are being discovered." In this sense the division of history into time, place, or thematic sections is very useful, even to the more mature student. But even the more mature student should be conscious of the fact that "the effort to divide history into periods is not free from certain dangers. It encourages the idea that great processes have a sudden beginning and come to an end with equal suddenness." History is an evolution because the progress of the race has not been by leaps and bounds but by slow stages; and yet the evolution of history, marked as it is by unity and continuity, must not be made so much a fetish as to lead the historian to disregard historical periods altogether.

History may be divided in many ways and from many points of view:

1. From the manner of its exposition, history has three forms—(a) the *narrative*, (b) the *pragmatic* or *didactic*, (c) the *genetic, explanatory*, or *scientific*.

2. From the extent of the subject-matter, his-

tory is either (a) *universal* or (b) *particular*.

3. From the standpoint of its character, history is either (a) *natural,* or (b) *supernatural,* that is, revealed history.

4. From the chronological viewpoint, the chief division of history is into *periods.* In the early Middle Ages, these periods were usually the six epochs as found in St. Augustine's *City of God*— from Adam to Noah, from Noah to Abraham, from Abraham to David, from David to the Babylonian Exile, from the Exile to Christ, and from Christ to the end of the world. Dionysius Exiguus is responsible for the systematization of these *aetates,* since he gave them a middle point or focus in the birth of Christ. The Greco-Roman theory of the four monarchies (Babylonian, Medo-Persian, Macedonian, and Roman), which was based upon the Book of Daniel (ii–27; vii–3), was the dominant periodization in the later Middle Ages and in earlier modern times. Since the time of Keller, the threefold chronological division in history has been kept: *Historia antiqua, Historia medii aevi, Historia moderna.*

Keller ended Ancient History with Constantine, Medieval History with Constantinople, and Modern History with the then present. These terminals have been more or less followed since his day. Their subdivisions are too well-known to need citation. Frederick Harrison gives their periodization in the following leading epochs and dominant phases:

a. The early Oriental theocracies.

b. The rise and development of the Greek world.

c. The rise and consolidation of the Roman world.

d. The Catholic and feudal world, known as the Middle Ages.

e. The formation and development of great European states.

f. The political and industrial revolution of the modern world.

"These dominant epochs," he writes, "should each be kept co-ordinate and clear in our minds, as mutually dependent on each other, and each as an inseparable part of a living whole. No conception of history would be adequate or other than starved and stunted, which entirely kept out of sight any one of these indispensable and characteristic epochs. They are all indissoluble; yet utterly different, and radically contrasted, just as the child is to the man, or the man to the woman; and for the same reason—that they are forms of one organic humanity."

5. From the religious viewpoint, history is either (a) *Church* history or (b) *profane* history.

6. From the standpoint of the material object, the thematic division of history is given by Feder (*Lehrbuch der geschichtlichen Methode*):

I. General History (Universal history, World History).

II. Special History:

    A. History of individual persons;

    B. Family or group history;

    C. Corporative history:

        1. Political history;

        2. Institutional history;

        3. Non-Political history (History of Civilization);

        4. Church History.

Probably a better division than any of the above is that which separates history as follows:

I. The history of what may be called *unique facts*. This is *General History* in the best sense, and is sometimes called *General Political History*, or *External History*. It tends to replace in our day the larger scope of *World History*. It is the *Allgemeine Geschichte* of the Germans and the *l'Histoire Générale* of the French.

II. The history of *facts in groups*, classified by species. This is *Special History*, or history that corresponds to the manifold diverse forms of social activity. Sometimes this is called the *History of Civilization*, the limits of which are not yet clearly defined. It comprehends all the phenomena of social life to the exclusion of political events. A confusion arises between the *History of Civilization* and *Kulturgeschichte*. The two are not wholly identical, though there is a tendency to use them as synonymous. Sometimes the *History of Civilization* is called the *History of Society* or *Social History*. Special History is also called the *History of Institutions*. Carlton J. H. Hayes has combined both these divisions in two volumes which he calls the *Political and Social History of Modern Europe*.

The subdivisions of Special History are as numerous as are the aspects of human life. Of these special aspects, the following may be considered the principal divisions of institutional history:

1. *Constitutional history*—the development of the state as contrasted with the external history of the state, or political history.

2. *Legal history*—the principles and development of law—public, administrative, etc.

3. *Economic history*—production, exchange, etc., as contrasted with sociology or the philosophy of social phenomena, social history, and the economic interpretation of history.

4. *History of literature, science, education.*

5. *History of art.*

6. *History of customs,* or *Social history*—the

history of society in a united sense, as contrasted with the *History of Civilization*.

7. *Religious history* or the history of religions
—this is sometimes taken as a part of social
history, while ecclesiastical institutions are
frequently considered as part of public and
administrative functions of the state or of
society.

Religious history in its widest meaning includes
the entire history of beliefs or of faiths from the
earliest known sources to the present. There is
but one division in religious history—the Incarnation of the God-Man. "The founding of the
Christian Church," writes Döllinger, "is the end
of an age-long preparation and development and
the beginning of a new world order. The world
before Christ and the world after Christ—such
is and such remains the simplest and truest division of history." Church history or ecclesiastical
history—the two words are practically inter-
changeable—is a part of general Christian
religious history, while all religious history before the coming of Christ—the Word of God,
the Way, the Truth, and the Life—can be
divided into pagan or Jewish history: the religious history of pagan peoples and the religious
history of the Jewish Dispensation or of the
Chosen People, from whom the Redeemer was
to come.

Christ Jesus, True God and True Man, is then the middle-point of all history. Godefroid Kurth has emphasized this fact in one of the attractive pages of his book, the *Church at the Turning Points of History*. "In the history of mankind considered as a whole," he says, "there are two grand divisions. On the one hand, there is the ancient world seated in the darkness of death; on the other, the modern world which advances in the light of the Gospel. This is beyond compare the greatest fact of history. The opposition between these two worlds is sharp and well-defined. The line of demarcation which separates them is very clearly drawn. It is not an imperceptible and gradual evolution that leads humanity from the one to the other. It is rather a new spiritual influence, a mighty impulse which brings about an immediate and radical change. We know the precise date of this great change, and we have taken that date as the starting point of our chronology. It is the Christian era that opens the annals of a new creation and a new humanity. . . . The principle of Christian civilization is essentially opposed to that of ancient society. Compare the two worlds: on the surface you will find many characteristics common to both, but at the basis of these common traits you will perceive the irreducible contradictions of the fundamental idea on which they are

founded.   It is a question not only of a difference
of degree, but a difference of nature, and this
difference has a bearing on the most vital interests of human life."

Ecclesiastical history has its centre in Christ
and in His Church.   We say centre, for the question arises whether there are limits of time or
limits of viewpoint to ecclesiastical history.
Collins has ably discussed the gamut of time included in the idea of Church history in his *Study
of Ecclesiastical History,* and quotes with approval Dean Stanley's method of including in the
scope of Church history the Church of the Old
Dispensation as well as that of the New.   Objectively, Church history begins with the first
man Adam, follows him and his descendants
down to the time of Christ, and in a more special
manner the religious life of mankind since the
coming of Christ to the present.   Church history
is the history of the Kingdom of God on earth—
of its origin and its progress from age to age,
during both the period of preparation before
Christ and of fulfillment after Christ.   Church
history in a less wide sense is "the history of the
foundation, nature, development and vicissitudes
of the Church of Christ, the regeneration of man
and his gradual union with God through Christ
in the Holy Ghost."   Church history, in consequence, is a universal history.   Before the

foundation of Christianity there was no universal
church, and it is with Christ, therefore, that universal Church history begins.

To understand fully the origin and development of the Church of Christ, the religious and
moral character of the world prior to the introduction of Christianity must be studied. "The
history of the Church," says Pascal, "ought
properly be called the history of truth." So also
does Bossuet in his sermon on the Divinity of
Christ characterize Church history—"c'est l'histoire du regne de la vérité." A recent writer,—
G. K. Chesterton, in *Orthodoxy,* has stated the
same thought in his own striking fashion:

To have fallen into any of those open traps
of error and exaggeration which fashion after
fashion and sect after sect set along the historic
path of Christendom—that would indeed have
been simple. It is always simple to fall: there
are an infinity of angles at which one falls, only
one at which one stands. To have fallen into
any of the fads from Gnosticism to Christian
Science would indeed have been obvious and tame.
But to have avoided them all has been one whirling adventure; and in my vision the heavenly
chariot flies thundering through the ages, the
dull heresies sprawling and prostrate, the wild
truth reeling but erect.

In this sense, the history of Truth must begin
with the first page of Revelation, since God, who

alone can reveal the mystery of the origin and destiny of man, has spoken to us by his prophets before revealing His Will through his Divine Son Jesus. The name *Church* can therefore in all justness be given to all those who have lived by these revelations and to all those who (according to the words of Pius IX), in spite of ignorance of revealed dogmas, but following the precepts of the natural law, are ready to obey God in everything and thus by virtue of divine light and grace are able to reach eternal life. If then, one takes the Church to mean the congregation of all the faithful who have believed in the true God, the Church has always been in existence.

Brugère, in his *Tableau de l'Histoire et de la Littérature de l'Eglise,* distinguishes three phases in the history of the Church. The first is universal in principle, but created to last only to the coming of Christ. This is the *patriarchal* Church, or the totality of men who have preserved the tradition of religious truth. The second is the local *Mosaic* Church, the theocracy, both spiritual and temporal, imposed upon the Jewish people and endowed with a special organization for the efficacious preservation of truth up to the coming of Christ. The third is the universal and perpetual Church, the *Christian* Church, or more properly called, the *Catholic* Church; namely, that spiritual society founded and organized to embrace all races and all times, and guided infallibly by the Holy Spirit for the accomplishment of its divine mission—the establishment of the Kingdom of God on earth.

The history of the Christian Church has for its object "to follow the fortunes and trace the progress of the Kingdom of God on earth." In a general way, this object has been more fully described as follows:

1. To state the circumstances, both favorable and unfavorable, under which the Church, by command of Christ, and after the manner of the mustard seed in the Gospel, sprang into life and *spread* to the ends of the earth, and how, by the energizing power of the vital principle within her, she leavened and renewed the world, and gradually came into contact with all nations, to which she stood in various relations.

2. To explain how a divinely constituted hierarchy in the Church, consisting of a primacy, an episcopate, a presbyterate, and a diaconate, necessarily called into existence an ecclesiastical *constitution,* which embraces the members of the whole body, assigns to each his appropriate place, and defines the rights and duties of all, and how the Church adapts her discipline to the requirements of every age and country.

3. To show how the Church, assured that she alone was in the possession of the deposit of saving and sanctifying truth, impressed the same conviction on the whole body ecclesiastic, and with special emphasis at the breaking out of

heresies; and how she has built up a complete system of *theological science* whose dogmas are marked with the same characteristic.

4. To point out how the Church, by her public *worship,* gave expression to her inner religious life, thus awakening and nourishing the piety of her children, and vindicating her divine origin and supernatural tendency.

5. To show how the Church instilled into her children her own instinctive hatred of sin, and set before them, with a view to their sanctification, the excellence of a religious and *moral life,* and in this way led them on to vigorous maturity of the full age of Christ.

6. Finally, to prove that through these influences she has shaped a *Church discipline* truly educational in character, meeting all the wants of every age and the only hope of society.

If our relationship towards the problems of history in itself as an object of study is today full of confusion, the case is, therefore, altered when we enter the field of Church history. There no hesitance is found either in the definition of the thing itself or in its divisions. All the definitions given in the countless Manuals and Compendiums are equivalent in terms and in meaning to the fundamental one: *Nomine historiæ ecclesiasticæ intelligimus scientiam et narrationem de vita interna et externa Ecclesiæ, de ejus progressu et ad conformandos populorum mores efficacitate.* It has been defined as "that department of history which has for its subject the Church or Churches that have been founded to promote man's supernatural interests." Alzog's definition, as given above, is considered a complete one. Brück, whose Manual held popular favour of Seminary and College teachers during the last generation, defines the object of Church history as follows: "To portray the spread of Christianity in the relation it bears to the various peoples on the earth's surface; as also to depict the interior development of the Church in regard to constitution, doctrine, and worship, as far as it is possible to do so." One of the latest Manuals, that of Funk, defines it: "Church history records the propagation and the preservation of the Christian religion, its boundaries, and the manifold vicissitudes and persecutions it underwent, and finally its relations with the different states of the world, some of which scornfully rejected the Gospel message, while others, even among those who were converted to Christianity, did not accept its teachings in a uniform manner."

All these definitions, influenced naturally by the theological background of the object embraced in the study of Church history, are based on the philosophical distinction of the outward and inward development of Christian society. The outward or external relationships of the

Church are those which record its extension throughout the world; its inner relationships, those which are concerned with the constitutional development of the doctrine and discipline of the Church.

There is, therefore, no vagueness about the definition of Church history, since every definition is necessarily centred about the external and internal development of the Church, and these are again divided into well-defined special aspects.

Thus the internal history of the Church views those particular ecclesiastical institutions which form the compact organization of the Catholic religious society—hierarchy of order and jurisdiction; doctrine and doctrinal development; discipline; worship and liturgy; Christian social customs or morals; and Christian devotional life.

External Church history treats its development *ad extra*—the propagation of the faith and missionary activity; relations of the Church with the State; influence of Christian doctrine and morals on public morals and social institutions; Christian influence in the realm of literature, art, science and material progress. Even non-Catholic Church historians accept this mode of defining Church history, though caution must be observed in their use of the word *Church,* since in most cases the word to them connotes an invisible as well as a visible Church; truth to them being objectively attainable in the invisible Church, but only imperfectly knowable in the visible Church through the light of history. Mosheim, the foremost Church historian produced by the Protestant Church, defines Church history in a way that can be readily accepted by the Catholic scholar who keeps this distinction in mind:

Ecclesiastical history is a clear and faithful narration of the transactions, revolutions, and events, that relate to that large community which bears the name of Jesus Christ, and is vulgarly known under the denomination of the Church. It comprehends both the external and internal condition of this community, and so connects each event with the causes from which it proceeds, and the instruments which have been concerned in its production, that the attentive reader may be led to observe the displays of providential wisdom and goodness in the preservation of the Church, and thus find his piety improved, as well as his knowledge. . . . The *External History* of the Church comprehends all the changes, vicissitudes, and events, that have diversified the external state and condition of this sacred community. And as all public societies have their periods of lustre and decay, and are exposed to revolutions both of a happy and calamitous nature, so this first branch of Ecclesiastical History may be subdivided into two, comprehending, respectively, the *prosperous* and *calamitous* events that have happened to the Church. . . . Its *Internal History* comprehends the changes and vicissitudes that have happened in its inward constitution, in that system of discipline and doctrine by which it stands distinguished from all other religious societies. This branch may be properly termed the *History of the Christian Religion*. The causes of these internal changes are to be sought for principally in the conduct ·and measures of those who have presided and borne rule in the Church. It has been too frequently their practice to interpret the truths and precepts of religion in a manner accommodated to their particular systems, nay, to their private interest; and, while they have found in some implicit obedience, they have met with warm opposition from others. Hence have proceeded theological broils and civil commotions, in which the cause of religion has often been defended at the expense both of justice and humanity. All these things must be observed with the strictest attention by an ecclesiastical historian.

It is to be regretted, however, that the clarity of the concept of Church history has not been preserved in its divisions. The division of secular or political history into three great periods was adopted by the authors of the Manuals and Handbooks of the last century and the tripartite method has not made for an intelligent survey of the Church's past.

Church history is either *universal* or *particular*:

I. *Universal Church history* embraces all the social groups which have composed the Church of

Christ from its foundation and all the manifestations of its external and internal activity.

II. *Particular Church history* on the contrary is limited to one or to the other branches or aspects of universal Church history.

In a loose sense universal Church history is sometimes called general Church history; as contrasted with particular Church history, or Church history viewed from any of the special aspects of religious activity. These special aspects can be classified in three ways—from the standpoint of the geographical or social groups within the Church, from the various forms of social activity within these groups, and from the chronological viewpoint. *Idea, place,* and *time* sum up the three methods; but in the two former, the last is never wholly ignored, since the classification of facts, genetically studied, must be regarded within the time-units of these facts.

Special history of the Church, viewed within the limits of geographic or social groups, gives us: the particular history of the Church in the various nations; corporative history; the religious history of one country, one region, or one locality. Special history of the Church, from the systematic standpoint, deals largely with its institutional growth and development, and may be divided into the following large sections: (a) history of public ecclesiastical institutions; (b) history of dogmas and heresies; (c) history of discipline and worship; (d) history of asceticism and devotion; (e) history of ecclesiastical science and literature; (f) hagiography and history of art; (g) the economic and social history of the Church. Special history of the Church, according to the chronological mode of its divisions, embraces the three epochs commonly known as Christian Antiquity, the Middle Ages, and Modern Times.

A. *Christian Antiquity* begins with the Birth of Christ, the *fulness of time,* and ends with the sixth or seventh century. It is the period of the origin of the Church. Its dominant and external note is the conversion of the pagan nations. Its internal history is that of the organization of the hierarchy, the formation of Christian discipline and worship, the subjective evolution of dogma, and the transformation of pagan morals. It is also called the Greco-Roman Period. Christian Antiquity is again subdivided into

> I. First Epoch—from the foundation of the Church to the Edict of Milan (313);
>
> II. Second Epoch—from the Edict of Milan to the Second Council of Trullo (313–692).

B. The *Middle Ages* are begun by many
Church historians about the sixth century
and continue to the Protestant Rebellion
in the sixteenth century. The customary
subdivisions are:

> I. The conversion of the barbarian
> nations to the death of Charle-
> magne (814).
>
> II. Politico-religious history (814–
> 1073).
>
> III. The rise of papal supremacy
> (1073–1303), during which time
> the Popes appear as presidents
> of the Christian Republic of Eu-
> rope—from Boniface VIII to
> Gregory VII.
>
> IV. The Decadence of the Chris-
> tian Republic of Europe (1303–
> 1517).

C. *Modern Times* begin with the Protestant
Revolt (1517) and come down to the
present. The main subdivisions are:

> I. The Church and the Protestant
> religious groups to the French
> Revolution (1517–1789).
>
>> 1. Religious wars to the
>> Treaty of Westphalia
>> (1517–1648).

2. Internal Catholic struggles—Jansenism, Gallican-
ism, Josephism (1648–
1789).

II. The Church and Infidelity (un-
belief, scepticism, rationalism,
materialism) from 1789 to the
present:

1. The struggle against rationalism and false liberalism (1789–1848).

2. The struggle against materialism and socialism
(1848–    ).

All these periods and epochs have been further
divided and subdivided until Church history becomes a veritable patchwork of design dazzling
the eye that traces its development from the
day of Pentecost to the present time. And yet,
without this scaffolding of divisions and subdivisions, the edifice of Church history can hardly be
built. No one method of grouping the facts of
Church history meets the difficulty. A perfect
synchronization is an ideal that cannot be
reached, even with the division into periods,
epochs and sections, since any two of these must
overlap and since none of them escapes the influence of contemporary non-ecclesiastical events

and institutions. The division into centuries as inaugurated by the Magdeburg scholars and by Baronius never won acceptance because it is a rigid mould into which facts of all kinds have to be thrust. A general history of the unique facts only of Church history would be Church history without a soul. A history of all the ecclesiastical institutions in a synthetic form would be unintelligible, even were it possible; and while it may be desirable to have monographs on each of the special aspects of the institutional life of the Church, no true idea of Church history could be given if important events are slurred in the process.

A combination of general and institutional history—or rather a juxtaposition of the two—in each epoch and period is apparently the nearest approach to the ideal; and hence practically all the Manuals or General Histories are so arranged. In the latest *General History of the Church*—that published by Fernand Mourret in ten volumes—the main divisions of the Christian era are as follows:

1. Christian origins;
2. The Fathers of the Church;
3. The Church and the barbarian world;
4. Christendom;
5. The Renaissance and the Reformation;
6. The *Ancien Régime;*

7. The Church and the Revolution (1775–1823).

8. The Church in Contemporary Times (1823–1914).

In each of these divisions, made according to subject-matter, it is the chronological treatment which rules the method of separation. Apparently of all "posts," as Hinsdale calls dates, before which the student stands "and throws his facts at them," two have assumed or have been given a larger importance than any others in Church History. These are 313—the Edict of Milan; and 1517—the beginning of the Protestant Revolt, or what was formerly called by historians, the Reformation.

Neither of these dates has in itself sufficient historic content to be emphasized as a principal milestone along the pathway of the past nineteen centuries of Church history. Historical scholars are not in accord on the essential value of the Edict of Milan as a turning-point in the religious life of Christendom. That it was a remarkable event in Christian history, being the first Edict of Toleration in the world, is admitted. It established the policy of viewing the Church as an institution distinct from the State. But these factors do not settle the question whether the promulgation of the Edict is of sufficient importance to warrant its use as a definitive date in Church history. Even the name *Edict* is apparently a coining of seventeenth century historians.

The bold act of Luther on All Hallows, 1517, in nailing up his 95 theses on Indulgences on the door of the Castle Church at Wittenberg, loses much of its boldness when viewed in the light of the movement for reform which antedates his birth by many decades. Nobody in Europe, says a recent Protestant Church historian, was more surprised than Luther himself by the outcome of his act.

That we need these two dates—313 and 1517 —and the many others which make up a divisional apparatus for the gradual initiation of the student into the detailed knowledge of Church history, is evident. Without some such stopping-places along the highway of the Christian conquest of sin and error, it would be impossible to make adequate and accurate retrospects and prospects for the journeying. But as in the study of history proper, all such divisions in Church history are makeshifts or purely mechanical means of approaching so universal a subject. The division along horizontal lines into centuries destroys the sequence of events. The horizontal division into periods, with general titles, such as the Apostolic Age, the Age of the Persecutions, the Barbarian Era, the Feudal Church, the Dark

Ages, the Middle Ages, the Reformation Epoch, is an improvement on the century-plan; but again it rends the seamless garment of Church history and confuses the orderly sequence of events besides compelling the student to wander from one subject to another and from one country to another without any logical reason. A third method is to divide Church history vertically instead of horizontally, that is to follow the Church history of each country separately. This method makes for continuity, but it robs the study of Church history of its most fascinating element —its universality. Moreover it violates the catholicity of action and life in the Christian Church.

There is a further factor in the method of approach towards the subject of universal history which adds to the student's difficulty—all religious history is part of universal Church history, and to exclude the study of any of the churches which claim to be the true Church or branches of the true Church is to truncate the subject at one of its most valuable points. All Christian churches not in communion today with the Roman See originated by secession from the Catholic Church. They are Christian and remain Christian only in so far as they have preserved within their creeds the doctrines and the discipline of the Roman Catholic Church. The Catholic heritage in modern Protestant Christianity is still a notable one, in spite of the disintegration and deterioration inherent in all heresy. "The Catholic historian does not admit that the various forms of the Christian religion may be taken, roughly speaking, as a connected whole, nor does he consider them one and all as so many imperfect attempts to adapt the teachings and institutions of Christ to the changing needs of the times, nor as progressive steps towards a future higher unity wherein alone we must seek the perfect ideal of Christianity. There is but one divine revelation given by Christ, but one ecclesiastical tradition based on it; hence only one Church can be the true one—the Church in which the aforesaid revelation is found in its entirety, and whose institutions have developed on the basis of this revelation and under the guidance of the Holy Spirit. To assume equality among the various forms of the Christian religions would be equivalent to a denial of the divine origin and supernatural character of the Church."

This distinction is highly important to the Catholic student of historical interpretation, since Church historical science has not been uninfluenced by the newer critical attitude towards the past. Each of the various interpretations of history has left its effect upon the study of religious history, and probably none has had a wider or more subtle influence upon non-Catholic Church historians than the economic interpretation of the religious progress of Christianity. The net result of one of the latest newcomers into the sisterhood of the historical sciences—the study of comparative religions—has also helped to undermine the divine character of the Christian revelation and has promoted the idea of the transitoriness of all religions and of the untenableness of the supernatural in the explanation of religious history. The Christian Church is viewed, therefore, as merely a further step away from paganism and the Jewish Dispensation towards another, a final, a more perfect religious development of the truth.

The Catholic historian is obliged to refuse compromise with this conclusion. His Church is the central subject of universal ecclesiastical history. All other churches, all other forms or expressions of the Christian religion, can only be regarded, in the light of their origin or foundation, as seceding bodies from the parent Church. The *reliquiæ* of Catholic doctrine which they still retain must enter into the Catholic student's purview; and the influences, direct or indirect, by way of persecution of the Mother Church, of ostracism of a social or a political nature of her children, of more definite statements on doctrinal and disciplinary questions, which the non-Catholic

Christian bodies caused through attack upon the parent Church—all these influences and many more which hardly need to be mentioned, create the necessity of a thorough knowledge of all forms of religion, if the external and internal development of the Catholic Church is to be fully understood by the student.

The student is now in a position to grasp the meaning and the scope of ecclesiastical history. That historical science displays at every turn in our days a vigorous, dynamic quality of development should not mislead the student into a sort of beatified optimism which shuts its eyes to the confusion that reigns in all these initial problems—definition, division, aims and purposes, method of treatment, and logical interpretation of the facts of history.   This very confusion at the outset is probably an asset for which the historian is not fully grateful.   In no science does the cautious and careful establishment of the facts require more prudence.   The Ciceronian dictum—*ne quid falsi dicere audeat; ne quid veri dicere non audeat*—was written for the historian, and not for the natural scientist, who has had the privilege of blundering towards the truth through a long series of mistakes and errors.

The Anglican Bishop Stubbs thus describes the ideal attitude of the Church historian: "History enables us to approach questions in which we are ourselves engaged with moderate and cautious treatment, to allow some of them to wait for solution, to determine others by the evidence of fact rather than by prepossession, and to let others alone altogether.   Historical investigation teaches us patience, tolerance, respect for conflicting views, equitable consideration for conscientious opposition; we see how very differently the men of a particular time seem to have read the course of events which appear to us to have only one reasonable bearing; we see how good and evil mingle in the best of causes; we learn to see with patience the man whom we like the best often in the wrong, and repulsive men often in the right; we learn to recognize that the cause which we love best has suffered from the awkwardness of its defenders so great disparagement as in strict equity to justify the men who were assaulting it.   We learn, too, and this is not the least of lessons, that there are many points on which no decision as to right and wrong, good or evil, acquittal or condemnation is to be looked for, and on which we may say that, as often the height of courage is to say, *I dare not,* and the height of love is to say, *I will not,* so the height of wisdom is to have learned to say, *I do not know.*"

# CHAPTER II

## THE SCOPE OF CHURCH HISTORY

Any attempt to give within a limited outline the main events of the history of the Catholic Church is beset with many pitfalls which are of necessity unavoidable. The height and the depth, the length and the breadth of the subject-matter of Church history have no counterpart. They are, like the Church itself, universal in extent. "From any point of view," writes Collins in *The Study of Ecclesiastical History,* "the Church is the most prominent and most significant factor in the history of civilized nations." The Church is to the world what the soul is to the body. No perspective of history can be excluded from the cosmic significance of Christianity; and "in the light of the Incarnation, out of which the Church flows, nothing human is foreign to its line of development." In Gwatkin's phrase, Church history is the spiritual side of universal history. How, then, can its subject-matter be limited? The very diversity of the personages, great and small; the places, near and remote; and the movements, good and evil, or, to use Mosheim's distinction, prosperous and calamitous, involved in the general religious retrospect of the past twenty centuries renders limitation of any kind almost impossible of achievement. The very unity of the subject-matter but adds to the historian's difficulty, since his rôle is primarily not that of the theologian nor that of the apologist.

To the historian imperative duties are: first, to ascertain the facts precisely as they happened, next, to interpret them in the way in which they happened with firm but delicate balancing of their causes and their effects, and lastly, to show their connection in the clearest possible fashion and with absolute sincerity. To the philosopher, the apologist, and the theologian, he must leave explanations, applications, and lessons, since these do not fall within his domain. Yet, how complex and baffling such a task becomes in the field of ecclesiastical history. The Church record is the world record. The master-key to open a hundred closed doors is in the former.

Limitations there must be in any narrative of the Church's past when proper balance, connection, and proportion of events are sought. To which aspect of Church history should the primacy of characteristics be given? Is it to the papacy, to that long line—the world's oldest dynasty—of sovereign pontiffs, from Peter to

the present Pope, who have ruled the Fold of
Christ and by whose authority and under whose
jurisdiction the messengers of the Gospel in all
ages—the priests and the bishops—have been
sent from Rome as from a centre to every corner
of the known world? Or, rather, is it not to
that complex, intricate, delicate, and fascinating
aspect of the Church's internal development—
her age-long and victorious struggle to preserve
spotless and intact the Deposit of Faith from
the sullying hands of error? Or again, should not
the high lights on the vast canvass of Church history be given to another aspect which can be
more easily understood from our coign of vantage
—the unchangeable law which has presided over
twenty centuries of Catholicism: the safeguard-
ing of the liberty and independence of the Kingdom of God from every human power that has
wished to enthrall it? These three main aspects
do not begin to exhaust the possibilities within
the stream of the Church's history, but they represent an initial difficulty to the student of religious history.

The Church has espoused the Eternal. In the
proud language of the Council of Trent, she is
"a standard raised above the nations" in order
that by it the presence of God in His earthly
kingdom be made manifest to men. Destined to
survive and to surpass the mightiest empires the

world has seen or ever will see, the Church is
the City of God on earth; and, in the words of
the Apocalypse, *the City hath no need of the sun
nor of the moon to enlighten it, for the glory of
God enlightens it, and the Lamb is the light
thereof.* How shall the development of this
City of God from its infancy in the Upper Chamber at Jerusalem to the present be narrated?
The question will never be adequately answered;
for, with whatever retrospective vision we gaze,
the epic grandeur of the Church unfolds itself
like a mighty panorama beyond the power of
any genius to describe with all its infinitely varied
details. "The influences of the Church vary in
extent and intensity—writes Bishop Shahan in
his *Study of Church History*—circumstances of
a political or social character widen or narrow
her field of action. The temperaments of peoples and the preoccupations of epochs, moral
degradation, suspicion and prejudice, mental and
material transformations of the world of human-
kind—a multitude of considerations affect her action within and without. In the person of an
Innocent the Third she might usurp the poet's
word: *Nihil humani a me alienum puto.* And
again, she might find herself relegated to the
narrowest margin of action and influence, the divine ichor in her veins barely flowing, an outlaw
in the eyes of societies that she had created and

made great. Then, too, her action is not always visible, measurable at first glance, so deep and wide wander the roots of spiritual forces, so subtle and unseizable are the impulses of the Holy Spirit."

Out of it all—out of the tremendous past of the Church, out of the certainties and uncertainties that crowd its pages, one fact looms high in historical value: if ever there was a power or an institution on earth which should long since have perished from the memory of man, that power and that institution is the Catholic Church. What has not been done to destroy it? A hundred times in the past twenty centuries has the Church of God stood on the verge of utter collapse. So has it seemed to human eyes. But the standard set up in the midst of the nations remains forever erect, strengthening its adherents with the unfaltering assurance that their faith is founded upon a rock, solid and impregnable. In its infancy in the Jewish synagogues of a dying Israel, amid the unspeakable perils of the Roman persecutions, in the depths of the catacombs, under the dead weight of the barbarian blight, in the subtle toils of feudal encroachments, in the presence of the mighty tyranny of a new Cæsarism, in the dark night of the cleavage during the sixteenth century, amid the enmities of Protestant nations and the uncertain friendships of Catholic nations, down to these days of our own, the struggle for liberty of action and independence for spiritual conquest has never ceased. But through it all and in it all and in spite of all that has been attempted to thwart the onward march of her progress, the Church has been victorious. *This, then, is the foremost lesson of her history: the unconquerable stability of the Catholic faith.*

From the very start, Christianity found itself in a state of crisis, a state of siege. The most immediate contact of the Church with the world about her was through what must ever be most closely connected with her: namely, other religions. The first enemy of the Church's liberty was Pharisaic Judaism. "Pharisaism meant the completion, Christianity the abolition of national Judaism." Stephen died that the Church's freedom might live. James, the brother of John, was beheaded; Peter was imprisoned; and James, the cousin of the Lord, was stoned. It was the beginning of the violence of the ages against the Spouse of Christ. From the soil reddened with the blood of the first martyr sprang the first conquest: the fuller consciousness of the Church's universality. And into the fold, on the very wings of the destruction he was contriving, came the greatest Apostle of all ages—Paul of Tarsus.

The first of these religious contacts brought out

more saliently than ever the fundamental law of Christianity—not altogether a law of continuity which binds the Church forever with Christ, her Founder, but a law of non-compromise. The Church is the eternal *non possumus* of the ages where truth is in the balance. In her conflict with Judaism both within and without her own ranks, she made her position plain beyond cavil: she has never taken up, she never can take up "the attitude of granting dogmatic toleration to religious systems as they are, by paying compliments to the truth that there may be in them and in making concessions to their errors. That is not like the Church."

At the outset, the truth she taught proved that she contained the whole of all future civilization in her very universality. No other religions were needed to carry on the work of the world's salvation. No other religions would be tolerated. There was but one Faith, one Lord, one baptism, one divine society, outside whose ranks salvation was unobtainable. All mankind was her child.

About the year of Our Lord 29, the Catholic Church existed in its essential fulness as a nucleus in the Upper Chamber. There were the Apostles, a few of the disciples and some of the faithful. Under the authority of its divinely appointed supreme head, Peter, the Prince of the Apostles and the first Pope, the Church was then fully formed and fully organized. It was in possession of a doctrine, complete, determined, unchangeable—a doctrine which would be preserved by sacredly kept traditions until it was confided, in part at least, to the written pages of the Sacred Books. Its sacramental system, those channels of grace which linked her forever to the great watershed of God's mercy and justice, had been wholly and entirely fashioned by the Master. The Church possessed divine power to exercise a salutary discipline over the faithful, to make laws for their life as followers of Christ, and to punish transgressions against His commandments.

With the dawning of the Day of Pentecost— the birthday of the Church—Judaism as a religious factor in the world's salvation no longer existed. Its work of preparation had been accomplished. For thousands of years, Judaism amid many perils had preserved belief in the coming of the Messiah and in his Kingdom. With the *fulness of time* upon the world at last, Israel and Christianity met to part forever. There can be nothing henceforth in common between them except the historic lineage which binds the first Christian congregations with the synagogues to which they had been accustomed.

The parting was not to be without conflict. The Pharisees without, the Judaizers within, were at one in this: that in their concept of the

Christian Church the new faith was to be but an episode in the religious life of the Jews. The former determined to exterminate the new faith; the latter to absorb it. The Church triumphed over both. This was her first grave problem, her first historical turning-point, the sublime story of which is told in the first Church history, the *Acts of the Apostles*. And the decision taken—to abandon Jerusalem in order to conquer the world that lay beyond—ends the first page of her history and begins another, a "mightier battle upon a vaster stage." With the baptism of the pagan centurion Cornelius, the independence of the Christian religion from Judaism was implicitly asserted. The Jewish clique within the fold was suppressed. The open road of the Empire awaited the messengers of the Gospel of Christ, messengers who were to preach the founding of an empire greater than Rome had ever dreamed and a citizenship in a new kingdom which was then upon the earth, with a doctrine and a discipline that meant the transformation of the very foundations upon which the pagan Roman state rested. The one institution which believed itself eternal was at last face to face with another which knew by divine teaching that it alone possessed immortality. In every conceivable way, in thought, in culture, in its understanding of the true, the beautiful and the good, the Christian faith was opposed in irreconcilable opposition to the Greco-Roman world. Never before in her history had the Roman commonwealth stood before so dangerous an enemy. To the pagan and to the Christian there was nothing in common. Life and death and the eternal verities were all involved. It was the young David matched against the strongest Goliath of all time.

"When the Apostles went forth to teach all nations the doctrine of the crucified Jesus—so writes Shahan in the *Beginnings of Christianity* —nearly all earthly power was possessed by the City of Rome. . . . How slow and uncertain might have been the spread of the Christian religion if its Apostles had been obliged at every step to deal with new governments, new prejudices, new languages. Hence the Christian Fathers saw in the unity of the Empire something providential and divine. . . . When St. Paul tells us: *Verily their sound hath gone forth into all the earth and their words unto the ends of the whole world,* he expresses a fact which the Christian society has looked upon as a historical marvel, a *prima facie* evidence of the innate truth and charm of the apostolic preaching." Under the pressure of a penal law system which outrivaled the most savage repressions in history, the Christian faith grew and maintained itself in the midst of the final insanity of paganism, the only just name for which is butchery. For three centuries, times of horrible persecution, followed by fitful periods of toleration, succeeded one another until the middle of the third century, when the word went forth over the empire that the new religion was to be exterminated root and branch. Decius (249–251) instituted this general persecution. Valerian (253–260) struck at the leaders, the bishops, priests and deacons, all Christian senators and judges, and prominent citizens who were members of the Church. To exterminate the organization of the Church and then to allow the masses to fall back again into paganism, such was Valerian's legacy to Diocletian (284–305), under whom the battle was to be one of life or death. No persecution before his time reached such height of fury; but it was all in vain. Seven years after his death, the decisive victory had been won and Christianity had triumphed.

The causes of the rapid spread of the faith were political, social, economic and religious. There was a perfect governmental system in the Empire. There was an easy access to all parts of the Roman world along the military roads. The common use of the two languages of the civilized world—Greek and Latin—made contacts with all classes possible. The inherent force of truth itself embodied in the Christian religion made its teaching efficacious in as much as its doctrines were above worldly wisdom and equally accessible to all men. No other doctrine offered so final and so satisfying a solution to those problems which had incessantly occupied men's minds—the question of God's existence and His nature, the immortality of the soul, life, death, and eternal justice. The power of the Christian faith to satisfy to the fullest the desires of the human soul; the miracles wrought by the Apostles and their successors; the zeal and the virtuous life of the early Christians; and the constancy of the martyrs—these are the salient points of the victory.

Within a hundred years after the death of Christ, owing to these and other causes, the Christian religion was universally known throughout the Empire. There was a kind of universal apostleship abroad in the Church. The Church was in reality a veritable army of missionaries. Against them the majesty and the power of the Empire had raised itself as a mighty giant awakening from slumber, and in ten great assaults strove to conquer this new force waxing strong within its borders. How many were slain in the conflict between a dying paganism and a life-giving Christianity no one can estimate. "By their death the ancient world was cleared of a thousand horrid bloody customs, institutions, and public vices. . . . At last, the taunt of the pagan was silenced—the God of the Christians did more than succor them. At Saxa Rubra by the Milvian Bridge, near Rome, the sun went down on one world, the world of paganism, and rose on another, the world of Christianity. . . . The era of the martyrs was like the first epoch of its vast career, and furnished the Church with an absolute and certain proof that the Holy Spirit was with her, that Jesus Christ was truly living and reigning in the world, that the Divine Father had not forgotten His children even in the furnace of tribulation. Those three centuries of severest trial stand out henceforth in the life of the Church as a cornerstone of fact, a bedrock of conviction, a pillar and foundation of her confidence in the final success of her mission, her teaching, her ideas."

The political conversion of the Emperor Constantine to Christianity was followed by the publication of a decree of toleration at Milan in 313, and with this decree, to which later ages gave the historic name, "Edict of Milan," there came an end to the three centuries of legal persecution of the Church. The Christian religion had now become a recognized religion in the Empire, and the first fruits of the Edict were the gradual abandonment of the catacombs as places of worship and the erection of new, or the transformation of old, basilicas for Christian services.    Among these was the Lateran, *l'église mère* of the Church.

The older Church history Manuals speak of the Milan decree as the Triumph of Christianity. Triumph there was, a triumph of martyrdom which brought recognition and religious toleration. But the idea of a general triumph must not be stressed too heavily. "It would give a false picture to represent the body of the Christians in the first three centuries after the type of those martyrs whose memory the Church has rightly glorified. The mass of the Christians then as at all times was cowardly, wavering in the faith, feeble in their profession before men, and incapable of resistance in the hour of danger. When persecution came, too many were ready to forswear their faith in order to save property, position and life. . . . And yet, the Church remained unconquerable. The marvel of Christianity and its greatest accomplishments is just this: that it could not be destroyed, that it won the victory although so miserably represented by its followers. Apostasy, weaknesses, and sin have had no power to destroy the imperishable strength of Christianity. . . . Through all the shades and darkness which surround us in the history of the Christian Church, there breaks evermore victorious—like the sun going forth in his strength, rending the clouds asunder and gleaming through the rift now in one place, now in another—the imperishable light of true Christianity. So was it even then. The Church conquered, not because of Christians, but in spite of them—through the power of the Gospel."

The Constantinian Peace can be taken as the chief transitional factor in the second—and longest—period of Church history, to which the much-abused name of medieval epoch has been given. A millennium was to follow, a millennium of lights and shadows, of glories and tragedies, the complete knowledge of which no man shall ever encompass.

Few of us come to the study of the Middle Ages without prejudices. Fewer historians have written about the Middle Ages without giving expression to these prejudices by too much or too little praise, too much or too little blame. It would be misleading to interpret the political and legal, the social and religious effects of the Constantinian Edict of Toleration as constituting a great rallying point in history for the weak and the courageous, the saintly and the sinful around the new Labarum set up within the Empire. What the Edict did more than anything else in these earliest decades of the fourth century was to give the Church of God a breathing place to look about her and to measure the mixed content of her victory, the mixed content of her progress. Four grave problems had confronted her from the middle of the second century:—a moral problem involving the original purity of the Christian life; a philosophical problem involving the appeal of Christian doctrine to the literati of the pagan world; a dogmatic problem centring about the problem of evil; and an apologetic problem that was essentially bound up with the propagation of the faith among all classes. To the first of these problems we owe the most highly venerated book of early Christian antiquity, the *Shepherd of Hermas*. To the second the answer was given by the noblest and purest convert from the paganism of that age, St. Justin Martyr, in his *Apology* and his *Dialogue with Tryphon*. The third problem, that of Gnosticism, the fruitful parent of all the heresies of the past, was easily the most dangerous of the four. It brought forth the first great Catholic work in systematic theology, the *Adversus Haereses* of St. Irenaeus, Bishop of Lyons. In the domain of apologetics, or explaining to the Jewish and pagan world outside the early Church the doctrines upon which the faith was based, certain names stand out as prominent in the transition years of the second and third centuries—Tertullian, Minucius Felix, the author of the Epistle to Diognetus, St. Cyprian of Carthage, and Origen.

All these works and many others of major and minor importance had clarified the doctrine and the constitution of the Church, had vindicated the unity of the Church and the primacy of the See of Rome, and had stimulated Christians of every walk in life to a fuller expansion of the social laws which bound them together into one vast organization. Works of benevolence, educational centres, intellectual activity, and holiness of living flourished side by side with the defections and the errors which had found a lodging within the fold. These works, discovered to the pagan world at the beginning of the fourth century how independent and how all-permeating the faith had become during the penal period. The fourth century, therefore, found the Church on the threshold of a long era, of extraordinary brilliancy. Guizot, in his *Lectures on European History,* has written this tribute to the centuries that follow:

From the fourth to the thirteenth century it is the Church which always marches in the front rank of civilization. . . . I must call your attention to the fact which stands as the head of all others, and characterizes the Christian Church in general—a fact which, so to speak, has decided its destiny. This fact is the unity of the Church, the unity of the Christian society, irrespectively of all diversities of time, of place, of power, of language, or origin. Wonderful phenomenon! It is just at the moment when the Roman Empire is breaking up and disappearing that the Christian Church gathers itself up and takes its definitive form. Political unity perishes, religious unity emerges. Populations endlessly different in origin, habits, speech, destiny, rush upon the scene; all becomes local and partial; every enlarged idea, every general institution, every great social arrangement is lost sight of; and in this moment the Christian Church proclaims most loudly the unity of its teaching, the universality of its law. . . . And from the bosom of the most frightful political disorder the world has ever seen has arisen the largest and purest idea, perhaps, which ever drew men together: the idea of a spiritual society.

If the Church became the Church of the Empire during this long period of a thousand years, if her power as the greatest force in Christendom for the transmission of ancient culture and the civilization of mankind was upheld by the State, therein was to lie all her strength; therein were to lie all the dangers of the next ten centuries. Henceforth, her enemies were to be those of her own household. It does not lessen the glory of her achievement during this long period to recognize that the paganism of the first epoch had not disappeared, living—as its very name indicates—out beyond the reach of busy Christian communities, watching alertly for every opportunity to penetrate the *Civitas Dei* of Christianity's making. As events proved, under various guises there were many within the City of God ever ready to follow new forms of Christianity, especially those which would include some of the pagan practices of the past or those which would look upon life less severely—a semi-pagan Christianity or a semi-Christian paganism. The greatest heresy of Christendom opened the medieval epoch; the next greatest ended it in the cleavage of the sixteenth century. Gnosticism and its multiform divisions, Montanism, Mithraism, the neo-Platonic groups, Manichaeism, and other errors found their first synthesis in the Arian hurricane of the early part of the fourth century. Arianism gave rise in the succeeding centuries to controversies and to heresies on the veriest fundamentals of the Christian faith; and the Church militant in those historic battle-grounds of the faith—the General Councils—met every doctrinal and disciplinary difficulty with a firmness and definiteness which have won the admiration of all succeeding generations.

As each of these doctrinal crises reached its climax in the Church, it was sifted to its very essence. The tide of infiltrating paganism was

turned back from the fold.   Freedom from doctrinal error and from excessive disciplinary
growth was gained, at times at fearful costs.   It
has been well said that the Middle Ages began
with a tremendous process of destruction.   The
earlier theological controversies, mostly of an
eastern origin, had not helped to weld the two
grand divisions of the Empire—the East and
the West.   The political division in 395 had
already separated, in body, at least, the two seg-
ments, and the first eight General Councils can
be viewed also as striving to preserve the political
along with the religious unity of the Empire.
But the end of the first conciliar epoch (325–
681) saw the ancient Eastern Church tottering to
its ruin.   Like a stream of fire devouring all life
before it, the troops of the Mohammedan conquerors had poured over Asia and Africa during the seventh and eighth centuries and were
battering at the door of Christendom in the West.
They failed at Tours, but in the East the Greek
Church was lost to Christian unity.   Councils of
reunion were held at long intervals, and the
Crusades gained a temporary victory, but under
Islam the Greek nation lost its life, and its great
Church of the seventh century "turned to stone."

We have come in recent years to a new valuation of that immense movement—the *Völkerwan-
derungen* of the fourth to the sixth centuries.

The old picture, graphically startling as it was—and so satisfying in its sharp outlines—of destruction coming upon the West on the wings of the night wind, the whirlwind of the hosts of the Teuton races swarming down upon the cities and towns of the Empire like wolves on the fold of Israel, destroying and laying waste all the heritage of the past—this can hardly give us an accurate simile of the events as they actually happened.   Come they did in great droves, like huge long lines of emigrants trekking their way to a newer and better land.   Land hunger was in their breasts, but when they came, it was not a new paganism that the Church had to cope with, but rather a race of giants, with a morality high above that of the masses of the Roman empire, brave and resourceful soldiers and captains at their head, anxious and eager to learn the best things the culture of Rome had created, and to some extent Christian in religion.

Before Rome "fell" under the barbarian weight in 476, there had been many ominous mutterings within the ranks of the Christian faithful who saw in the impending doom the end of the Church.   The universal empire and the universal Church were united in the minds of Christians. To them the end of Roman civilization was the end of the world.   When the day of shame and of mourning came and the Eternal City was

violated by the outrages and sacrileges of the barbarians, even the comforting pages of the *Civitas
Dei* which St. Augustine had penned in those de-
clining years of the ancient civilization to teach
his people that the Church would live after the
World had fallen, were barely heeded.

There are few more tragic pages in the history
of Rome.   But the Christian Church understood.
Standing upon the watch-towers of Israel, the
Mother saw the dawn of a new civilization, and
undaunted, conscious of her eternal mission, she
went "to those who were then the heralds of
destiny, and, her hand in theirs, she took the road
to the future."   The Empire had fallen; the
Church remained.   The world was in ruins about
her, but as the embodiment of all that was best in
the past, the Church set out upon a rescue that
would end by making the very conquerors conquer
themselves.   At the hands of her missionaries,
the Teuton races from the Tyne to the Danube
caught up her message of sweetness and light, her
cry of warning of the world to come; and upon
the fusion of the two races—Teuton and Latin—
the Christian Church was to build a new Empire
with which she would share a title sacred to herself for centuries—Holy.

Upon the ruins of the old Empire the Church
built as never before nor since in her long history.   Only in these latter days has the medieval

period of the Church's religious life come into its own glory and recognition. No longer do historians follow blindly the false guidance of the humanists, who pictured the thousand years of the Middle Ages as a long night set down from the skies, a long silence between the *Götterdämmerung* of the pagan world and the golden age of the Renaissance. The old Voltaireian flings at the alleged despotism, the ignorance, the barbarian culture of those centuries, are now forgotten. Even that one word which caught up all this disdain—Gothic, has become a term of praise for matchless beauty. The multitude of monographs, books, source-collections and archeological discoveries of this and the preceeding generation of scholars has discovered the Middle Ages as a period of prodigious intellectual activity. We know better today the splendid chain of elementary and secondary schools, the cluster of noble universities, and the marvellous intellectual life of the Church from Charlemagne to Petrarch, and thence into the Renaissance, which in its Christian aspects is but the flowering of the ages behind it. The incomparable political and social activity of these middle years of the Christian era are nowadays the admiration and the pleasure of a host of scholars who recognize how profoundly the Church carried the spirit of Christianity into the making of laws and into those guarantees for individual liberty upon which social harmony within the nations was based.

No generation recognizes so clearly as ours the political, and therefore the economic and social, values of the federation of these nations which the Church formed for international peace and justice. "The five centuries in which was effected the conversion of central, northern and eastern Europe offer a striking spectacle. Christian virtue was brought home to millions of men who had never risen above the ideal of animal courage. In the persons of apostles and saints of both sexes, a spiritual world was opened up that gave employment to the crushed or famished instincts of the heart. Woman, the slave, the captive, the child, the failures even of barbarian society, appeared in the new light transfigured as brethren of Christ. A host of new ideas clamored for expression in the vernaculars of semi-savage tribes. The Roman private law, so equable, rational and common-human in its spirit and provisions; the canon law, so evangelical and other-worldly in its scope and method, perfected or modified their rude customary usages and procedure. A certain detritus of ancient culture was preserved as a sacred fire, which would one day quicken into medieval literature and art. The Church itself was now just such a society as was needed by the barbarian tribes: motherly and compassionate, where they were rude and violent; universal, where they were splintered into infinite sections; refined, where they were coarse and uncouth; related intimately to all past history, peoples and civilization, where they were but emerging from their forests. In these centuries they learned what virtue was when practised by the Christians: their own institutions, like feudalism, took on something of Christian mildness and mysticism. Then was seen that rare phenomenon, an apostolic nation, in the persons of the thousands of Irish missionaries who flooded Central Europe, while their disciples and imitators, the Anglo-Saxons, were scarcely less active and devoted. In the latter half of this period bloodshed and force appear as unchristian and deplorable elements of persuasion—a crusading spirit that was often worldly-calculating, and saw in the baptism of the pagan tribes the sure renunciation of old national or racial independence or opposition. Nor could this vast work be done without some concession to the popular passions or traditions, as they lived on in pagan superstitions. They were gradually eliminated or allowed to live on under forms that did not seriously affect Christian principles or doctrine. That there is a certain unity in this long missionary movement is owing to the direction and influence of the Roman Church, to which, mediately or immediately, are referable the impulses that brought these Northern nations into the Church."

To accomplish all this, a threefold policy was needed by the Church; or, rather, one and the same policy with three effects upon the world it sought to conquer for Christ. The first was the strengthening of the Church at its centre. This was an initial task and one in which both Popes and princes coöperated. The primacy of Peter in doctrinal matters is now recognized as having never been called seriously into question in the ancient and medieval Church. From out the supreme authority of the papacy in disciplinary affairs there was to grow up about the Church a temporal power which remained a basic idea in medieval life from the time of Charlemagne to the end of the thirteenth century. During these years the Pope and the Emperor, the head of the Christian Church and the head of the Christian princes, "stood in intimate relation to each other, and the Papacy and the Empire are in a sense the central points about which the history of the West during the whole of the Middle Ages moves." It is, moreover, in this intimacy of the spiritual and the temporal that all the grave problems of Church life take their origin and in which the germ of all that was good and of much that was fatal to the liberty and independence of the Church is to be found.

Once the power of the Holy See had been solidly established, the Church was free to send out without danger, since they journeyed under the protection of the Emperor and the Christian princes, those warriors of the Gospel, the second great race of Apostles and Disciples, whose prototype must ever be St. Boniface, the Apostle of Germany, into all parts of Christendom. They completed their work quickly. Then came the task, which only the Catholic Church has succeeded in accomplishing, and that but once—the federation of the nations into the Christian Republic of Europe.

The first apex of success in this triple policy came on Christmas Day, 800, when Pope Leo crowned Charlemagne as Roman Emperor. The ninth and tenth centuries—the real Dark Ages of the Church—were to follow; but even in the sombre hours of this sad night of evil, there stands the figure of one of the greatest Popes of all times, Nicholas I (858–867). Historians are wont to see in this middle period of the medieval epoch the Church surrounded by a triple menace—the peril of imperial vassalage for the papacy; the peril of feudal encroachment on the Church's liberty, when the Roman people themselves balanced the two supreme powers, imperial and papal, against each other for their own political ends; and the Byzantine peril, which grew out of the hatred Constantinople and the East bore this Empire not of its own making. Probably the most striking fact in the history of this Age of Iron, as Baronius calls it, is to see one of the most unworthy of all the Popes, the young John XII, receive Otto as the saviour of Rome (962) and place upon his brow the imperial crown of Charlemagne.

The remaining centuries of the medieval epoch are so crowded with the struggle between the Empire and the Papacy, that many writers have been misled into making the Holy Roman Empire the central thread of medieval history. There is much more than this conflict, which assumes a normalcy that is highly disconcerting to the student, in the years that followed Otto's crowning to the end of the epoch. Many of the evils the Church had to eradicate from the fair field of Christendom grew out of the encroachments of the temporal power over the spiritual, and out of the disturbance of the balance of power the papacy held in the hierarchical organization of the Church. Lay investiture was a crying abuse. A simoniacal priesthood was another. An incontinent clergy was still another, and a worse, evil. Heretical doctrines, echoes of the pantheism and rationalism of earlier ages, such as the

Cathari, the Albigenses, the Waldenses, and other minor sects, added to the confusion of the times.

To remedy these disorders, a reform was necessary; and the inexhaustible vitality of the Church became visible in that life-giving stream of sanctification which began to flow at this time from the monasteries, particularly from that of Cluny. "These monks of Cluny," writes Sohm, "with their mortified bodies, with their glowing eyes and haggard faces, became the saints of the people; for in them the Christian ideal as conceived by the Middle Ages, had become again alive. The peasant sunk in coarsest sensuality saw here, in bodily form before his eyes, the spirit of Christianity which triumphantly overcomes this world of earth. The monasticism of Cluny became the centre of a powerful and enthusiastic movement. . . . In this new-born monasticism there lay the force which gave to the Church a new inner life, which won over large classes of the population to the Church's ideal, which delivered the Church from her subordination to the temporal power, and brought forth the age of the medieval hierarchy."

In Popes Sylvester II (999–1003), St. Gregory VII (1073–1085), Innocent III (1198–1216), and Boniface VIII (1294–1303), the spirit of reform in all departments of ecclesiastical life and in all aspects of Christian perfection saw its dominant years. During these pontificates, the Church won her independence from the tyranny of imperial overlordship. She limited with consummate tact and forbearance the tendency of the imperial power to interfere in purely spiritual affairs. She went farther in her determination to safeguard her liberty as the supreme spiritual law-giver, by codifying her Canon Law. She gave new life to European unity by the rôle she played in the Crusades.

But, granting that during the twelfth and thirteenth centuries the Church became to all practical purposes the supreme authority to Western Europe, the struggle for her complete liberty was not ended. Even in these years, when the Holy Roman Empire of the German Nation ceased to be the turbulent source of conflict with the spiritual sovereignty of the Church, another nation, which had come out of the Crusades with a glory unrivalled in Europe, France, began its long and inglorious history as the dissolving force which brought the Christian Republic of Europe to an end.

In the struggle between Philip the Fair of France and Boniface VIII, the medieval ideal of Christendom met its most dangerous enemy: the theory of the omnipotent State, the source of medieval and modern absolutism—the work

of the jurists of the French Court. These
*légistes* or *chevaliers-ès-lois,* setting up the old
Roman law as a fetish, began the attack upon the
chief institutions of the Middle Ages (custom,
the right of property, the feudal contract, and
Christian royalty); and from this attack came
the worst foe the Church has had to face then
or since—neo-Cæsarism, or the absolute State.

After the fall of the Hohenstaufens, the jurists
found a fruitful soil for their doctrines at the
Court of Philip the Fair. "It is well to note
the origin of royal absolutism in Europe. . . .
We are at the antipodes of the Christian theory
of power. The principles formulated by Philip
the Fair were those which the Popes opposed and
defeated in their struggle against the Hohenstaufens. They were those which would henceforth be invoked wherever there was question
of humiliating or belittling the Holy See, or,
whenever, despite the resistance of the Holy See,
there was question of encroaching in one point
or another upon the patrimony of Christian public
right bequeathed to the nations by former ages.
And it is worthy of remark that a great number
of historians, followed by a veritable mob of
second-rate minds, persuade themselves with a
naïveté almost ludicrous, that these theories of
royal absolutism are Catholic doctrines. . . .
From a national point of view the absolutism of

kings broke the equilibrium of the social body, concentrated all the life in the head, atrophied free institutions and made revolution the only possible corrective of tyrannicide. . . . The Catholic Church, seated at the foot of the Cross, waits calmly for the day when revolution shall have finished the education of mankind."

The papacy was now face to face with this new danger. Conflict was inevitable. In the six centuries that have passed since Boniface VIII strove to avert the catastrophe by those great messages, *Clericis laicos, Ausculta fili,* and *Unam Sanctam,* written between 1296 and 1302, the situation between Church and State has been one long drawn-out combat, the end of which is not yet in sight.

Boniface VIII is the last of the medieval Popes. With his successor, Benedict XI, the modern epoch of Catholic history begins, and it is an epoch of rebellion against the past. Events were now to follow in quick succession as Europe strode forward towards revolution. The outrage at Anagni (1303) was followed two years later by the election of Bertrand de Got, Archbishop of Bordeaux, to the papal throne; and as Clement V, this French subject of an English king began the Avignon period of the Papacy, which goes in history under the name of the Babylonian Captivity (1305–1378). It is

needless to dwell on the effect of this translation
of the Holy See to an insignificant city on the
Rhone.   Even Mollat, the latest author on the
subject, in his *Les Papes d'Avignon,* endeavors
to find a favorable reply to the general condemnation of Church historians against this French
period of the Papacy, but is silent on the grave
effects of the Captivity.

Side-by-side, or rather, hand-in-hand, with the
wreckage of the Christian Republic caused by the
jurists went the equally serious rebellion of
heterodox leaders, such as William of Occam,
Marsilio of Padua, and John Wycliff.   In their
writings it was the spiritual power of the Papacy
which was attacked.   Almost one might say, in
all reverence, that the papacy had fallen and that
the *coup de grâce* was given during the half-
century which followed Avignon, when Western
Europe beheld a schism to which it has attached the cognomen: Great.   During these years
(1378–1417), the Christian Church was divided
between two and sometimes three spiritual obedi-
ences, and while the election of Martin V (1417–
1431) restored unity to the Church and the
Holy See to Rome, the spiritual prestige of the
Papacy was to suffer as during no other epoch in
its history in the pontificates of those Popes
whose reigns mark the transition between medi-

eval and modern times, and who are known as the Popes of the Renaissance (1458–1521).

How far the Renaissance was the work of churchmen and how far it was the result of purely pagan influences is still a debatable question. It is, of course, a capital error in history to regard it as an abrupt and sudden resurrection of intellectual life after ten long centuries of darkness. That would be to forget the learning of the Middle Ages, the universities, scholastic philosophy and theology, the art and the architecture, the painting and the music, the sculpture, the natural sciences and the poetry of the medieval period. In history there is no effect without a cause, and the Renaissance is but the natural, progressive evolution of the intellectual life of the Middle Ages, and not, as is so often stated, a revival of learning caused by the influx of Greek scholars after the Turkish invasions.

It is well for the student of Church history to view the intellectual, political, social, economic, and religious transitional movements, which today are known under the names Humanism, Renaissance, Commercial Revolution, Protestant Revolt, and Catholic Reformation, not as separate or distinct factors in the marvellous sixteenth century, but rather as interweaving or interpenetrating elements of one general change.

The character of the times was manifestly changing, but in what that change precisely consisted it would be hazardous to state. Nothing is more fatal to the proper understanding of any historical epoch than to accept simple explanations for its achievements. The use of simple terms as if they contained a synthetic value for the varied elements of such a tremendously passionate time in history as that which bridges medieval and modern ages is always misleading. The commonest of these terms, *Revival,* is the weakest. To distinguish the Renaissance as a revival of letters and the Protestant Revolt, its counterpart or consequence, as a revival of religion, is to take the line of least mental resistance in explaining their genesis and growth. The Renaissance was not wholly secular and classic; the Revolt was not essentially religious and moral.

The commercial revolution at the beginning of the sixteenth century had far-reaching effects upon the political conditions of Europe, and these in turn find their expression in the rise of democratic towns and in a new nationalism which saw the consolidation of four nationalities— England, France, Spain and Portugal—within their own borders and with them the end of the imperial unity of Europe. Perhaps the most striking factor after 1500 is the change this situation brought into papal policy—the beginning of the era of Concordats with individual princes and nations in place of the older system of the *entente* between the Church and the Empire. The friction which had always been in evidence between the *Imperium* and *Sacerdotium* during the entire medieval epoch could not fail to become acute when the Popes were obliged to treat not only with separate political powers, but also with the spirit of intense national consciousness or of absolutism dominating these powers. When this friction passed from the temporal to the spiritual order, all that was needed was the advent of a genius who would unite the two in a final revolt against the Church. That genius was the Augustinian monk, Martin Luther.

Whether or not Luther was the conscious agent of the politico-religious rebellion against the papacy is not a profound question to answer. What is of importance to the Church historian is the realization that the heart of the Middle Ages was essentially Catholic; and it comes very close to the truth to be told what "the world of the Middle Ages desired in its innermost heart was not *renaissance* but *reformation*—not the regeneration of art and learning, but the regeneration of the Church in its head and all its members; not the glad tidings of the re-discovery of the ancient world, but the glad tidings which are preached to the poor, which can bring blessedness to the sinner, and regenerate all mankind. Moral renaissance, through the renewal of the Christ's life—this was the greatest and highest aim for which the forces of the fifteenth century were stirred again and again in one united movement."

The series of events which cleaved asunder united Christendom from 1517 to 1648 are too well known to need recapitulation. The rejection of a central moral authority in Europe gave free rein and voice to a hundred discontents. Complaints and protests filled the air until all hope of stemming the flood of abuse which was to sweep over the papacy was abandoned. Into the whirlpool of rebellion every element of civilized life was caught and submerged. "For a while it seemed as if all the bonds of social order were broken—the reformers themselves stood aghast at the seething flood they had let loose." The dread harvest reaped by the peasants stands out in the fearful pages of Janssen's *History of the German People since the Close of the Middle Ages*. Liberty—if the freedom the Protestant Rebellion won can be justly called by so sacred a name—was gained at a price for which the world still pays an ever-increasing and appalling tax.

"The lifetime of Luther," writes Shahan, "was the darkest hour in the history of the Roman Church." Everything seemed lost—faith was apparently abandoned, authority flaunted, discipline made a by-word, and the great edifice of Catholic life and thought, reared by patient hands through a thousand years, was crumbling before the strong and sullen winds of the Rebellion. The old historic remedy—a General Council of the Church—was to be applied only in 1542. Through the pontificates of four Popes, to the year 1563, the Council of Trent sat in judgment upon the abuses which had been allowed to gain an abode in the Church. Catholicism was saved; but the old order had passed away forever. The seamless robe of Christ's Church was torn and parted. Christendom was divided into two warring camps of Christians. The cleavage had gone to the very roots of the religious life of the world.

Between 1520 and 1570, three distinct churches with fundamental doctrines in common—Lutheranism, Calvinism, and Anglicanism—gained religious control of practically one-half of Europe. In the remaining one-half the true reform was carried to its legitimate end by the Council of Trent and by those religious elements which compose the Counter-Reformation. The founding of the Society of Jesus by Saint Ignatius of Loyola, the reforms carried out in the regeneration of older Orders, the Carmelites and Franciscans, and the rise of new religious societies, dedicated to the instruction and training of the clergy, to the spiritual education of the people by means of missions and similar work, to the training of youth, and to the care of the sick, gave an unparalleled impetus to the faith in Europe. It was the age of St. Pius V, St. Charles Borromeo, St. Francis Xavier, and St. Teresa. Scarcely any age of the Church contains so brilliant a galaxy of saints and scholars.

Beyond the confines of the Old World, a new zeal was awakened, which was to bring millions into the Fold. Every force in the vast system of Catholicism felt the new life coursing through its veins, and in the lands brought into the ken of men by the discoveries of the period, these new millions "were being won as the raw material for another conquest of faith." India, Japan, China, the islands of the sea, a new world across the Atlantic, were soon the scenes of busy missionary groups; and, although the new conquest did not have any appreciable effect upon the worst disorder of the times—the breakage of religious unity, there was in the realization of this spread of the Gospel a consolation that sustained the Church throughout her tragedy.

During the seventeenth and eighteenth centuries the work of the Catholic Reformation continued, marred, it is true, by the introduction of a semi-Protestantism which assumed various forms: Jansenism, Gallicanism, Quietism, and Philosophism. With their history is intimately linked the movement which culminated also in the suppression of the Society of Jesus, and clearer light has been thrown in our days upon the link which binds the abolition of this supreme educational body to the French Revolution. The Renaissance can never be separated from the French Revolution, for all the currents of the latter catastrophe had their source in the spirit of free thought which the former had crystallized into a philosophy. Voltaire was the genius who synthesized all the irreligious spirit of the centuries which separated him from the jurists of Philip the Fair's reign; and from him came the century's watchword—*Écrasez l'infâme,* which summed up the century's hatred for Christianity. When Jean Jacques Rousseau carried this hatred to the masses, the Revolution was but a matter of time.

The first serious reaction to the rationalistic and infidel spirit of the Revolution came in the Romantic movement of the early part of the nineteenth century; and under the stimulus of its adherents and leaders, a new and more enlightened attitude towards Catholicism and towards the golden age of the Catholic Church was created and bore men on the crest of its current towards a renewed enthusiasm for religion.

"The powerful historic grandeur of the Papacy, the mighty and authoritative fabric of the Catholic Church, the pomp of Catholic worship which pressed all the arts into its service, all this exercised over Romanticism an irresistible magic. The Catholic laity burned again with ardor for their Church; nay more, a great number of leading Protestant Romanticists, like Stolberg, Phillips, Frederick von Schlegel, Zacharias Werner and others, went over to Catholicism."

The nineteenth century is called the century of democracy, the century of nationalism, the century of liberalism, the century of social revolution, the century of labor, the century of science. Between these aspects or ideals and Catholicism, historians generally see elements of dissent and opposition, the chief effect of which has been in their judgment the separation of the Church more definitely from the world; or at least to make her a tardy follower in the wake of modern intellectual and scientific progress.

On the surface of things, such a judgment can be sustained with apparent plausibility. But there is one factor in the history of the century which brings first hesitation and then a different conviction to the student. The nineteenth century, and more especially the first two decades of the present century, have changed the political

outlook, and that change involves the growing
necessity of viewing all history as world history.
Colonial questions have long since brought the
far ends of the earth nearer together. The en-
trance of Japan into the field of European civilization, the rapidly growing leadership of the
United States in the domain of commerce and
finance, and the levelling of barriers of many
kinds during the great struggle of 1914–1919—
all these have given a sense of unification of purpose to the world. That there is no unity between the greater and lesser political powers only
intensifies the points of contact wherein the world
finds itself, almost in spite of itself, united.

All this is far, very far indeed, from the unity
Christendom once enjoyed in the heyday of its
power. But all unifying movements of an international kind mean the establishment of closer
contacts between the millions who are members of
the Catholic Church and likewise a sense of freedom and security to the Church as a whole, which
was so sadly lacking from the Renaissance to the
Revolution. At the turn of the tide away from
the Terror, the Catholic Church brought to the
new nationalism the policies the world needed
to follow, if civilization was to be saved from the
wreckage of the French Revolution. Catholicism could not compromise with the principles of
the Revolution. No matter how sharply the

spirit of the age found itself in contrast with the doctrines of the Church, the vital difference between Catholicism and Atheism could never be bridged by compromise. So, too, were Catholic leaders to find the situation during the Liberal movement of the middle part of the century. Liberalism in its religious aspect meant far more than in its political bearings; and the Church in the person of Pius IX made her stand against it distinct and uncompromising.

During the pontificates of the four last Popes —Leo XIII, Pius X, Benedict XV, and Pius XI—the Church has neglected none of the principal intellectual and social movements of the times. But her real work has been outside the political, social and intellectual field. It has been, in an all-important way, confined to *the religious restoration of the world*. Any general judgment upon the success of that restoration would be premature. The series of state papers issued by Leo XIII will be the text books for a century to come. The encyclicals on Socialism, on the working classes, on Christian marriage, on liberty, on Church history, on biblical studies, on scholastic philosophy, and on Church and State, have been the highest inspiration to the Catholic scholarship of our times. They form an encyclopedia of Christian doctrine on all the problems raised by the infidel principles of the

French Revolution. As each one of these encyclicals appeared during the long reign of Leo XIII (1878–1903), they not only contributed to the intellectual, social and religious movements of the day but actually gave back to Catholic scholars a leadership which the world has sorely needed against the forces of Socialism, Communism, and atheism.

The Church of the present day has this striking feature in her position in the world—she presents at once under a hundred different aspects all the problems which have come to her in the course of her history. The Church today is in a large way a general picture of all the forces making for and against her universality, her liberty and independence of action, and her marvellous spiritual vitality. Undoubtedly, living as we do under the standard of papal infallibility, we are more than ever the inheritors of all the ages preceding our own. All the past belongs to the Church. All the future lies in her history. In a recent volume entitled *The World's Debt to the Catholic Church,* James J. Walsh has caught up all the strands of the civilization of the past and has traced their origin and growth within the Church.

No one will deny that the Catholic Church is the highest moral authority in the world today. She alone has preserved the right and the freedom to speak to all men. "She has but to raise her voice and from all parts of the universe she is answered. Today there is such a thing as Catholic thought, which measures all things by the rule of Christian truth, condemning what is opposed to it, accepting what is not hostile. Strong and respected, conscious of its power, it circulates from one end of the world to the other—no longer can any sophism withstand it. In sociology, in science, in art, in all manifestations of the intellectual and moral life of the people, Catholic thought asserts itself with increasing force and energy. It is opposed only by the conspiracy of silence. . . . Despite all contrary appearances we need not doubt her final triumph. The human soul is naturally Christian—everything great and good gravitates towards the Gospel. Human society is instinctively drawn in the direction of Jesus Christ whenever it obeys the law of self-preservation. The spirit of evil may do its worst, it will but precipitate events and hasten the day when humanity will have choice only between Catholic civilization and revolutionary anarchy."

Such, in epitome, with many silences unavoidable in so swift a description, is the province of ecclesiastical history. Historically speaking, the American world of intelligence and culture does

not know the Catholic Church and is indifferent
to the great long sweeping centuries of her external and internal life.   The history of the Church
is one of America's fascinating heritages from
the past.   Anything like a profound knowledge
of the Church's story is admittedly beyond the
powers of most students, and so the frost of neglect lies upon it.   The spirit of our age is not to
persecute the Church as in ancient times, not to
protect her as in medieval days, but to ignore
her.   In consequence, her history is ignored; but
the indifference towards her magnificent past is
not wholly in the minds and hearts of those who
are not her own children.

In his *Confessions of a Convert,* Robert Hugh
Benson has penned a remarkable summary of
Church history: "I saw the mystical Bride of
Christ, growing through the ages from the state
of childhood to adolescence, increasing in wisdom
and stature, not adding but developing her knowledge, strengthening her limbs, stretching out her
hand; changing indeed her aspect and her language, using now this set of human terms, now
that, to express better and better her mind; bringing out of her treasures things new and old, which
yet had been hers since the beginning, indwelt by
the Spirit of her Spouse, and even suffering as He
had done.   She, too, was betrayed and crucified;
dying daily 'like her great Lord; denied, mocked,

and despised; a child of sorrows and acquainted with grief; misrepresented, agonising; stripped of her garments, yet, like the King's daughter that she is, all glorious within'; dead even it seemed at times, yet, like her natural Prototype, still united to the Godhead; laid in the sepulchre, fenced in by secular powers, yet ever rising again on Easter Days, spiritual and transcendent, passing through doors that men thought closed forever, spreading her mystical banquets in upper rooms and by sea shores; and, above all, ascending forever beyond the skies and dwelling in heavenly places with Him who is her Bridegroom and her God."

# CHAPTER III

## THE VALUE OF CHURCH HISTORY

It is one of the commonplaces today that no period in the life of mankind has shown more intense interest in historical questions than our own. Scarcely any science or any part of science escapes the curiosity of the historian. The scholar who is unfamiliar with the detailed historical past of his chosen field of activity can only glimpse partially into its future. The primary influences which have created this profound insight into the value of history as one of the most constructive schools of human progress are too varied to be included in a single synthesis. The critical historian looks back a generation to find the foundations of his scholarship in the German university system of historical seminars. The historian of the Catholic Church sees an equally important stage in critical scholarship in Pope Leo XIII's letter on historical studies, written in 1883.

No change in collegiate or university circles during the past forty years is so marked as in the increased attention paid to historical study.

Fifty years ago, one would look in vain, even in our leading educational institutions, for a teacher devoted exclusively to the science of history. Canon Scannell could write in 1908: "Thirty years ago no branch of ecclesiastical study was so neglected as Church history. At the great Roman College only four half-hours a week were devoted to it, and these for only two of the four years' course of theology. The professor was a saintly man who spoke beautiful Latin. The text-book was supposed to be Wouters' *Historiae Ecclesiasticae Compendium*, but hardly ever was any reference made to it. A man might take a brilliant degree, and yet know little or nothing of the history of the Church. No wonder that the history lectures were shirked by all who could get out of attending them. And this in Rome, the very home of history."

Since these lines were written, history has penetrated every avenue of ecclesiastical science and has taken its rightful place as a major subject in the Church curriculum. Nowadays, in our colleges and universities, history is one of the leading branches and the historical department is usually as well staffed as those of law and letters. This change has affected the secondary and elementary schools, public, private and parochial; and while the same confusion reigns in estimating the value of Church history as an educational force as exists in history proper, we are gradually coming towards the light, although the leaders are still seeking a solution for the problems inherited from former generations.

One has but to read the reports of the Madison Conference (1892), of the Committee of Seven (1898), of Eight (1908), of Five (1911), and the Second Committee of Eight (1921) in the *Reports* of the American Historical Association, or the recent (1924) *History Inquiry,* to realize the serious unrest there is in history teaching. Professor Edgar Dawson has used the only phrase expressive of the situation—*the confusion of tongues.* If this field of teaching is in sad confusion, at the mercy of scattered, unorganized effort, a similar situation reigns in the domain of ecclesiastical history from the elementary Catholic school on through the high school, the academy, the college, the university, and the seminary. One fact is naturally agreed upon: the educational value of history. But even this result is nearer our own day than is generally realized. Professor Henry Johnson has summed up the various objects of history in his chapter on the question of aims and values in the *Teaching of History.* But his answer is a composite one, as is also that given by Henry E. Bourne in his excellent manual on the *Teaching of History and Civics.*

The question: Why should we teach history in schools? Why should we teach history at all? is posed also by Dr. Hinsdale in his *How to Study and Teach History,* a new edition of which came out in 1914. In a much more pointed way, the question may be asked: Of what value is the study of Church history? Has it any value at all in the Catholic school curriculum? Is it of value to anyone else except the theologian? Should it be of interest to the political and social historian? What is the principal advantage of Church history to the student of other branches of knowledge—to other branches of ecclesiastical knowledge? Can the historian of nations and governments, the biographer of great men of the past, the student of law, of medicine, of statecraft, of literature, of art, and of the sciences, find anything in the pages of Church history that will throw additional light on his own investigations? Is it possible, finally, for the philosopher, the lover of wisdom, to ignore the history of the Church?

Hinsdale—and many others who follow him without giving credit to his work—answers the more general problem in a way that may help us to see better the value of ecclesiastical history in particular. Since all studies, he says, may be divided into four groups—the instrumental, the practical, the disciplinary, and the cultural—

history, if tested by these four aspects, responds with alacrity to each of them. History is an instrumental science, since no science is complete today unless its history is known. It is a practical science, both mentally and morally. It is a disciplinary science—was it not Cicero who called it "the witness of time, the light of truth, the mistress of life"? And in the gamut of the culture-giving sciences history ranks among the highest. It aids in the formation and possession of moral character. It strengthens the ability of the mind to analyze and to think logically. It is in itself the best means of acquiring a quantitative content of knowledge, whether of a general kind leading to broad mental outlooks or of a special kind leading to scholarship. It awakens a power of expression and an ability to coördinate the judgments of the mind. And its study strengthens in the scholar intellectual habits that are necessary for further mental and moral development.

If all this be true—and there are prominent educators, among them Herbert Spencer, who deny these claims for historical science—if all this be true only in a limited degree, then the study of that organization or society, founded by the Redeemer to lead mankind along the road of life to eternal happiness, undoubtedly has values yet unknown to the Catholic scholar. In his *Lectures on the History of the Eastern Church,* Dean Stanley has a much-prized chapter on the advantages of ecclesiastical history study. "Whatever may be the uncertainties of History," he writes, "whatever its antiquarian prejudices, whatever its imaginative temptations, there is at least one sobering and enlarging effect always to be expected from it—that it brings us down from speculations and fancies to what at least professes to be facts, and that those facts transport us some little distance from the interests and illusions of the present. This is especially true of History in connection with Theology. As it is one of the main characteristics of Christianity itself, that alone of all religions it claims to be founded on historical facts; that its doctrines and precepts in great measure have been conveyed to us in the form of history; and that this form has given them a substance, a vitality, a variety, which would, humanly speaking, have been attained in no other way; so we need not fear to confess that the same connection has existed through all the subsequent stages of the propagation of religion."

Almost all the Manuals or Handbooks of Church History of recent years devote a section or a chapter to the necessity and value of Church history. Bishop Shahan has given us an eloquent summary of its value in his excellent brochure on *The Study of Church History.*

More recently, there appeared from the pen of
a nun of Roehampton an admirable analysis of
the value of the science in *The Teaching of
Church History;* and some years ago there was
published by Abbé Blanc a volume entitled
*L'Introduction à l'Étude de l'Histoire Ecclésias-
tique,* which answers the question from the standpoint of philosophy and the theological sciences.
De Smedt has not touched the problem in his
*Introductio Generalis ad Historiam Ecclesias-
ticam,* though his *Principes de la Critique Historique* may well be called a general answer to the
question of the aims and purposes of scientific
Church history.    The best manual we possess up
to the present—Nirschl's *Propädeutik der Kirchengeschichte* gives a sturdy *plaidoyer* for the
science; and an excellent chapter on the subject
will be found in Solimani's *Importanza della
Storia.*    All these authors abound in references to
earlier literature, and hardly one fails to quote
the famous passage from Melchior Cano's *De
Locis Theologicis:* "That a theologian should
be well versed in history, is shown by the fate of
those who, through ignorance of history, have
fallen into error. . . . Whenever we theologians
preach, argue, or explain Holy Scripture, we
enter the domain of history."    The great Domin-
ican is echoing St. Jerome's words: *Multi
labuntur errore propter ignorantiam historiæ.*

No more striking appeal to the priest to make Church history his own particular domain of study has ever been written than the following passage from Bishop Shahan's little book:

I might say much more of the utility of Church history,—how it refines the spirit of the priest, and makes him largely tolerant and patient, by unfolding to him the incredible extent of human weakness and the mystery of God's triumph over it; how it is eminently suggestive of plans and schemes for actual good; how it breaks the awful impact of scandal by showing that evils come through neglect of law, obedience, charity or patience; how it consoles by the examples of saints of every condition, and instructs by the writings of holy churchmen, and delights by the growth of all the arts under the influence of the Christian spirit. Its influence on the theologian is great, as a man, a Christian, a student, a priest. As a man, he learns from it that the Church he serves has ever been the friend and uplifter of humanity, and has stood as a wall of brass against oppression and injustice; that slavery and barbarism have withered before its tread, and that Cæsaro-papism and blighting Islam have been warded off by it alone from our Western society. As a Christian, he learns a broader, more discriminating charity from the sight of so much human weakness, so much discrepancy between graces and deeds, office and conduct, the "fair outside and foul within." He learns the almost irresistible power of circumstances, early training, climate, topography, prejudices, inherited

trend of thought and character.   As a student his
judgment may be trained to a quasi-mathematical
precision by acute observation, his mental vision
may be so sharpened by practice as to discover
shadows and outline, and motion and life, in what
seems deep night to ordinary men——

The dark backward and abysm of time.

He may mete out, with incredible nicety, the
human and the accidental in ecclesiastical affairs;
the malice and the intention, the ignorance, the
stupidity, and the great undefinable margin of
causality that no one can fairly name or describe,
since its workings are hidden with God.   As a
priest and leader of the people, it multiplies and
deepens his sympathies, brings him out of the
abstract and theoretic into touch with the iron
realities of life, and accustoms him to see the
shaping hand of God, like the weaver behind his
loom, creating fairest patterns, though the ordinary looker-on observes nothing but din and disorder.

"To open the mind, to correct it, to refine it,
to enable it to know, and to digest, master, rule,
and use its knowledge, to give it power over its
own faculties, application, flexibility, method,
critical exactness, sagacity, resource, address,
eloquent expression," has even been counted the
specific purpose of any liberal teaching.   None
of the ecclesiastical sciences is better fitted than
the history of the Church to exercise such a
direction on the mind of the student.   The course
of events, "old in its texture, but ever new in

its coloring and fashion," is like a genial old pedagogue, with mind well stored and heart ever young and unspoiled, under whose mild and beaming eye the hearts of his pupils are as wax. If the object of knowledge on the part of the priest be, with St. Bernard, "to edify and to be edified," then there is none better suited to the churchman than the history of the society to which he belongs.

The preëminent value of Church history finds its adequate explanation in the object of the science itself. Church history deals with no dead past, but with the living present. The Church is a living organism. It is the mystical Spouse of Christ. From another point of view, it is a kingdom, old as the everlasting hills, but ever young, vigorous, fresh, and contemporary. Its four marks or characteristics of identity contain within themselves that universality of growth which leaves distinctions of time and space out of the synthesis of its development. It is a living thing, still imbued with its original power of expression, still young with the vitality of the days of its founding. It always was, either in the long years of the preparation for the establishment of the Kingdom of God on earth, or in the fulness of time which brought its Founder, or in its great stretch of the Christian centuries; and it always will be, until the end of time, for even the Gates of Hell cannot prevail against it. The

Church has no old age, because it has the eternal spark of life ever within its breast.   Its force has infinity of conquest and infinity of power.   "At no epoch," writes Sertillanges, "has the vitality of the Church ceased to manifest itself by new acquisitions.   She has suffered losses, like the living being whom sickness or a painful operation deprives of a limb: but she has amply repaired them. The number of her adherents has never ceased to grow.   The power of truth that is in her; her marvellous adaptation to the laws of life that makes her the most human and practical of institutions just because she is divine; the attraction of the unlimited hopes which she permits; the amount of desires which she satisfies, of natural aspirations for which she provides an adequate and even a superabundant goal; all this is enough to bring to her continually such beings of desire as we are."

By virtue, then, of its very object, Church history deserves a place high up among the sciences, and the first place in the historical sciences.   The greatest event in all history was the Incarnation of the God-Man; and the next greatest in the light of destiny was the Redemption of mankind and the founding of the Church to perpetuate the work of the Atonement.   Religion is the all-important thing in this world, and every religion, save the Catholic religion, lacks some essential thing. "Either they are ignorant of God, like the pagan religions, or they are ignorant of men, like Protestantism, which makes an individual of him, whereas he is a society; or they are ignorant of the real relation between God and man, like Buddhism, which desires to unite us to God by suppressing ourselves. And so of the others."

No other subject then possesses so strong a fascination for the scholar as the history of the Catholic Church. The Anglican Bishop Stubbs fell under its spell so completely that he feared to write about its value, lest he preach a sermon on the printed page. "The subject," he says, "is a very great subject; embracing every sort and department of details and principles, philosophic, theological, moral as well as historical; it is a subject that has a hold on us, not only through our minds, but on our heart and affections; it is one on which there is a desperate, almost internecine conflict between schools and sects; in which what to one set of men are principles to another are prejudices; what to one are fundamental truths are to the other fables little less than blasphemous; and it is one of itself full of stumbling-blocks and pitfalls, dangerous to all, most dangerous to those who, in soundness of heart and sincerity, think that the balance of truth and virtue and infallibility must always be on their own side. Like all History it has its grand lessons of patience, of suspended judgments, of tolerance and humility; and, like our own national history, it is full of temptations to read it always in our own sense of political fitness. The wisest man, accordingly, considering the subject-matter, has need to approach it with prayer and in faith: the earnest petition for guidance and that certain confidence, in which humility rests, waiting for the solution of hard questions; not dictating the way in which they must be answered, but certain that they will be answered in the appointed time:— and yet not the patience which, because the questions cannot be answered, will not deign to ask them; such is rather impatience or contented ignorance; but that which will try, as the law of the Church's life and progress reveals itself, in experience and development, to justify the wisdom of the Lawgiver, and, without anticipating consummation, accept, as sufficient for the day, the day's instalment of growing knowledge."

The importance of ecclesiastical history may be viewed under three phases. From the formal point of view, no study contributes more largely to the harmonious development of the mental faculties. The memory is enriched, not mechanically with long lists of dates and names, but with remembrances of moments in the historical past, with *souvenirs* of causes and effects in critical passages of that past which the historian can call upon at a moment's notice to illustrate his theme or to direct his judgment to present conditions.

A well-stocked memory with logical, chronological, and geographical classification of facts, with ideas that quickly associate themselves to cognate facts, and all these brought into unity, is one of the richest gifts for the work of historical synthesis. Intellectual memory is not an untrustworthy faculty of the mind; and although it needs to be carefully watched, the historian cannot disdain its special function of reproducing and recognizing facts and their correlatives gathered up in the course of his study. It is true that up almost to our own day history has been largely a work of the memory, and a burdensome work at that. But this does not beget a need to apologize for its use. The discipline of the memory is of supreme value to the mind, and an undisciplined memory is a common failing with many historical students. "The human memory is a delicate piece of registering apparatus," but unless it be exercised judiciously, it may be a burden rather than a mental asset. It is always an instrument of varying precision, and therefore to be followed cautiously.

Imagination is a second mental faculty which can play a valuable rôle in historical study. The relations between exact science and imagination have always been the subject of dispute, and there is a natural aversion on the part of the critical historians to its use. But no one will deny its great value in the reign of original research or in that of historical construction. Mark Baldwin has said that the imagination is "the prophetic forerunner of all great scientific discoveries." It is needless to point out the danger of a too fertile imagination in the historical sciences. Such danger is not common to history alone. In historical study, imagination has a place all its own in creating hypotheses for gaps between documents, gaps in the documents themselves, and gaps or *lacunae* between the facts of the source-material at the historian's disposal. "To put one's self in the place of a person who lived a thousand years ago, or even a hundred, or fifty years ago, to call the past to life even in its most commonplace aspects, to experience even a slight sense of reality in reading history, is work for the imagination."

Frankly, the difficulties in the use of the imagination are very great; and so are the chances for erroneous conclusions. But both the memory and the imagination are to be held in check by a third mental process—that of reasoning. In reasoning the safeguard to both will lie; for the student's work if critically done, will be but conclusions educed from proved historical premises and conclusions in the works of those who preceded him. Reasoning is the foremost essential instrument of the historical sciences. History is not a science based on direct observation. From facts already ascertained and authenticated, further facts are devolved by inference, and if the inference is guided by strict adherence to the laws of critical reasoning, then our historical knowledge of past events, places, or persons can be said to have moved forward. "But experience shows that of all the methods of acquiring historical knowledge, reasoning is the most difficult to employ correctly, and the one which has introduced the most serious errors."

That the value of the study of Church history lies to a large extent in the disciplinary and formative virtue it possesses for the training of these three powers of the mind, need not be stressed, for this value is the lowest in the scale. A higher value of Church history is that it furnishes the mind with a knowledge of the Christian past which is essentially encyclopedic in character. "Without ecclesiastical history," says Hergenröther, "there can be no complete scientific knowledge of Christianity."

It is Church history which tells us the story of the origin of Christianity; it is Church history which has preserved the narrative of the hierarchical institution of the Church, of its literature, its art, its doctrinal development, its worship and its discipline. It is Church history which demonstrates the action of the Christian spirit upon social, civil and public life, and in the growth of institutions cherished by our generation. No part of the progress of the world—material, intellectual, or moral—has been uninfluenced by the Church. In a more intimate manner, the value of Church history lies for the Catholic in its apologetic purposes. History is not an apologetic, and Church history used solely in an apologetic way ceases to be such. But the apologetical value of the science can hardly be exaggerated in these days when positive theology has won a place of equality with speculative theology. Church history, moreover, cannot escape this utilitarian influence; for, the past which it describes, is today the object of attack from materialistic and rationalistic thinkers who deny the divine, the spiritual, or the supernatural in their explanation of that past. Protestant Church historians who admit the supernatural in history deny that the Catholic Church is the same as that founded by Jesus Christ and assert that Protestantism is, or was, a return to the original purity of the Christian faith. It is to Church history the apologist and theologian must go for the refutation of this error. Only in the pages of Church history can a satisfactory explanation be found for the schism of the eastern Churches; and in many cases the only barrier protecting the

Church from false liberalism in its own ranks are the undeniable facts of history.

The anti-Catholic historical attitude is hardest of all to reverse, based as it is to so appalling an extent on ignorance of the Church's past, or on prejudices which crowd the lesser intelligences of the non-Catholic world. *Les préjugés se vulgarisent.* The truth is that the contribution of the Church to the civilization of the past and hence to the present is not known; and in that lack of definite knowledge must be justly included thousands of the Church's leaders between whose belief in the Church and love for the Church on the one hand, and whose knowledge on the other hand of the Church's twenty centuries of vigorous, active, spiritual regeneration of the world there is a bridge yet uncrossed.

The philosophical value of a general knowledge of Church history will consist to a great degree in its broadening influence upon the student. Knowledge and wisdom, as the poet Cowper says, far from being one, have ofttimes no connection. Historical study brings a practical wisdom from the past; and perhaps in no phase of the present is wisdom in judging more necessary than in the domain of the Church's historical past. "Knowledge comes, but wisdom lingers." Of the two elements in the development of Church doctrine and discipline—revelation and tradition—it is Church history which guards the traditions of the faith and cherishes the method of its transmission. In this way Church history is the treasury of the wisdom of past ages, and what is perhaps the most obvious value of this preservation is its guardianship over the truth. Like the terrestrial paradise, the whole history of the Church is an Eden of joy to the searcher after the truth. Pascal, in his *Pensées,* defines Church history, as has been said, as the history of truth—*L'histoire de l'Eglise doit être proprement appellée l'histoire de la vérité.* Christ came to establish the reign of truth, and the Church He founded is the divine custodian of that truth, since it is built upon Him —the Way, the Truth, and the Life.

In the theological training of her spiritual leaders for the priesthood, the Catholic Church teaches that truth in a seven fold ray, like a gleam of white light diffusing itself through a prism. Dogmatic theology proves the Church to be the depository of revealed truth and systematizes the deposit of faith entrusted to the Church to hand down to all generations. Pastoral theology describes for the priest his share in this work of transmitting the Catholic and Christian tradition of revealed truth. Moral theology explains the laws of God and of the Church, the channels of grace and the hindrances thereto.

Canon Law collects, correlates, and coordinates the laws of the Church. Ascetical theology is the science of Christian perfection, while Mystical theology treats of extraordinary degrees and forms of the soul's communings with God. Scriptural theology is that part of the general science which deals with the exegesis and hermeneutics of the Bible.

Of all these branches of the ecclesiastical sciences, dogmatic theology receives most directly its illumination from the pages of Church history. It is here that the symbols and creeds of the faith have been preserved. As century follows century, the student will find the belief of the Church dogmatically developed by the definitions of Councils and Popes and theologically developed in the writings of the Fathers and Doctors of the Church. Church history is the irrefutable witness to the identity of the faith of the twentieth century with that of the first century. It is in the annals and chronicles of the Church that the long, unceasing struggle made by the faith against heresy and persecution is told with all the objectivity of historical truth. The doctrinal development of the faith, writes Bishop Shahan, "is unintelligible without a knowledge of Church history. Without that knowledge we are liable to fall into one of two extremes, either to deny any development whatsoever, and thus lay ourselves open to the charge of ignorance and fanaticism, or to overstep the lawful limit and maintain a heresy . . . The student of the doctrines of the early Church must resign himself to become acquainted, to some extent, not only with Church history, but with profane history, with the history of Greek and Latin literature, with archeology, profane and ecclesiastical."

The current of Catholic theology has never been the same since the religious revolution of the sixteenth century.  The sudden rise of Protestant theology found Catholic theological science at one of its lowest levels, and the doctrinal content of the new religion was such that Catholic theologians had grave difficulty for a time in reaching a proper orientation for the defence of the faith.  It was likewise a period of low ebb of interest in Church history.  After 1570, that is, after the work of the Tridentine theologians began to exert its beneficent influence on the Church, Western Europe found itself divided between two Christian intellectual forces.  That division has not yet been bridged, in spite of the great syntheses of Leibnitz and of Bossuet and in spite of the reunion movement of this and the former generations.

What is of particular importance in understanding the depth of religious cleavage is the fact that the new heresies gave rise to a renewed interest in positive theology, as a complement to speculative and apologetic theology. In his *Origines de la Théologie Moderne*, Humbert writes: "De Bellarmin à Bossuet, dès décrets de Trente aux décrets du Vatican, le plus puissant levier du developpement dogmatique est la volonté avouée, ou secrète, ou inconsciente, de renforcer sur tous les points le système catholique contre les affirmations essentielles de la réforme." That reinforcement came principally from the students of ecclesiastical history who followed in the path marked out for them by the Father of Modern Church History, Cardinal Baronius. And it does not detract from the glory of the great apologists and controversialists, like Stapleton and Bellarmine, to acknowledge Bossuet's *History of the Variations of Protestantism* as the end of one epoch and the beginning of another in the doctrinal *certamen utriusque ecclesiae*.

Positive theology has passed through several crises, the last of which was during the Modernist errancy; but the historico-dogmatic school has gained so many successes since the Vatican Council that every phase of theology has been influenced by its force and suavity. In his *Théologie Catholique au XIX^e Siècle*, Bellamy describes these successes of the new school—the

publication of texts; the discovery of the *Didache;*
the archeological finds of De Rossi and his successors, Wilpert, Armellini, Marucchi, and
Kraus; the critical study of historical development in the doctrinal fields, as exemplified in
Batiffol's *Études d'Histoire et de Théologie
Positive,* in Duchesne's *Liber Pontificalis* and his
*Origins of Christian Worship;* in the histories of
dogma, especially that by Tixeront; and, what is
perhaps the greatest service history has rendered
to dogmatic theology, in the more perfect knowledge we possess of the traditional bases of the
faith.

Christian piety finds in the pages of Church
history the highest motives and stimulus, the most
perfect models and examples of Christian virtue.
The lives of the Apostles and disciples, the
*passiones* of the martyrs, the long weary years
of the persecutions, the attacks upon the faith
by the most brilliant leaders of paganism and
of heretical groups, the numberless exiles of
popes and bishops, the confiscations of the
sanctuaries of God, and the story of such outstanding struggles for the supremacy of the faith
as were made in Great Britain and Ireland
from Elizabeth's day to Catholic Emancipation
(1558–1829)—these are facts which quicken the
hearts of the faithful, encourage them in their

days of stress and conflict, and carry them along in the wide gulf stream of the Catholic triumph for Christ.

Had Church history never recorded these glowing pages, had those who were watchers on the towers of Israel during these epochs never written, how fruitful a source of Christian perfection would be wanting to the faithful of our day? The monastic ideal in the deserts, on the hillsides and among the mountains, and in the midst of busy civic communities, and the angelic life led by those innumerable holy women who consecrated themselves to Christ in Christian perfection, teach today through the voice of Church history, as they always taught, the Christian virtues of justice, charity, chastity, patience, and obedience. Take the knowledge we have of the historical surroundings away from those greatest spiritual books after the Bible— the *Imitation of Christ,* the *Exercises,* the *Way of Perfection,* the *Interior Castle,* the *Spiritual Combat,* the *Introduction to a Devout Life,* and *Sancta Sophia*—and much of their directness in fashioning the spiritual life of the reader is undoubtedly lost.

Ecclesiastical history is like a universal world-map, dotted all over with the rich and varied and sometimes puzzling experiences of the Church in the work of adapting her discipline to every

age, every class in society, and every nation in
the past.  Like the voice of the prophet, Church
history proclaims the Spouse of Christ as one
crying in the wilderness of this world the eternal
law of life—*Prepare ye the way of the Lord in
your hearts.*  Throughout the long centuries, the
Church has been making straight and true the
paths of the world of men in order that Christ's
doctrine may have easy and fruitful access to
their hearts.  Valleys of sin and scandal and
shame have been filled with the gentle and re-
freshing balm of her corrective discipline.  Hills
thrown up in barrier by the pride of the world
have been brought low, and the crooked and subtle influences of pagan ideals in social life have
been made straight, and the rough ways of dis-
content and rebellion made plain.  The Church
lives and moves and has its being for one ideal—
that all flesh may see the salvation of God.

In prophetic retrospect, Church history abun-
dantly tells this story of the past.  The work of
the ministry of souls confided to the bishops and
priests—*Ars artium regimen animarum*—does
not consist solely in simple spiritual direction: it
partakes of the very essence of Christian government.  For this reason, the study of moral
theology, as Bouquillon wrote a quarter of a
century ago, cannot fail to fall exceedingly low
in the scale of ecclesiastical sciences, unless it

be vivified by a careful examination of its historical past. The spirit of the historical method has not yet conquered the field of moral theology, and the average theological student—to quote a comment from that conservative review, the *Civiltà Cattolica*—is at the mercy of "a mass of compendiums made and fashioned with a somnolency almost senile, without a trace of profound study or exact criticism." There can be no correct account of the modern transformations of non-Catholic Christianity without a detailed history of the shipwreck of moral theology within its ranks.

The history of catechetical instruction, of homiletics, and of parochial management is also part of the general study of moral theology. The history of moral theology has never been adequately written, and without this knowledge, students must ever be at a loss to trace the evolution of many social and industrial problems of our own day. Since the Reformation, the social sciences have progressively lost contact with the Gospel of Christ, and the sociological movement so much in vogue today needs the historical background of moral theology for its explanation and correction. With the tendency to confine moral law more and more to private life, and with so many ethical problems tending to confuse the popular mind, there is needed a profound study of the development of moral theology as a basis for a Christian solution of these fatal tendencies in social and public life. ✓

In the other ecclesiastical sciences, especially in patrology, in canon law, and in the study of Holy Scripture, there is much that is practically identical with Church history, and in its pages the student will find the various causes which brought about their progress and kept that progress in harmony with the divine character of the deposit of faith. There he will recognize the harmony and continuity of the Church's teaching; here he will see the far-reaching social influence of the Church's legislation; there the earliest proof of the primacy of the Holy See; here the growth of the hierarchical constitution of the Church; and here and there, verily like sands on the seashore, the precious words and texts which carry us back to the days when the Evangelists heard and obeyed the inspiration of God. As page after page of her story passes under his eyes, the student will realize, to quote Stubbs' eloquent thought—that the Church is no mere idea, "but a reality of flesh and blood, wood and stone, books and words, souls and bodies, hopes and memories, loves and longings, sorrows and joys, sins and repentances, wanderings and returnings, experiences of example and accumulations of influences, developments and differentiations; a reality of men and women, a body with a life and limbs, nerves, sinews, fibres, joints and circulation; of heart and brain; a body 'growing up into Him in all things, which is the head, even Christ; from whom the whole body fitly joined together and compacted by that which every joint supplieth, according to the effectual working in the measure of every part, maketh increase of the body unto the edifying of itself in love.' Church history then becomes the tracing out of the 'working in the measure of every part,' in the past and in the present. Need I say more in illustration of the dignity and vital interest of the study to all who have the instinct of searching?"

There is another—and an unfortunate—aspect of the value of Church history which cannot be passed over in silence, especially since, as this chapter has endeavored to show, the duty of knowing Church history rests so seriously upon the Catholic priest: it is the conscious and intelligent recognition that, after the use of the sword and of legal persecution, no stronger weapon was fashioned during the earlier stages of the Protestant Rebellion than the misuse of Church history. In the hands of the Protestant Magdeburg Centuriators, the sanctuary of Church history was violated by profane robbers, stripped of all its beauty, and converted into an arsenal of slander against the papacy. From that day to the present, there has been in vigorous existence a pragmatic Protestant use of Church history for which the only just name is anti-Catholic.

Too frequently this unpleasant term is thought to apply only to movements which never rise above the sordid game of politics or spoils, or to historico-literary productions which batten on the less attractive moral side of Christian life. But the anti-Catholic frame of mind is not confined to the unlettered masses; it finds followers in the highest ranks. No better example of this frame of mind could be given than the following passage from Morley's *Life of Gladstone:* "Among the names which Mr. Gladstone was never willing to discuss with me was Joseph De Maistre, the hardiest, most adventurous, most ingenious and incisive of all the speculative champions of European reaction. In the pages of De Maistre he might have found the reasoned base on which the ultramontane creed may be supposed to rest. . . . In dealing with De Maistre, Mr. Gladstone would have found a foeman worthier of his powerful steel than the authors of the Syllabus, Schema, Postulatum, and all the rest of what he called the Vaticanism of 1870. But here, as always, he was a man of action, and wrote for a specific though perhaps for a fugitive purpose."

A recent writer has summed up the twelve basic defects of the anti-Catholic historical literature of our day as follows:

1. Anti-Catholic history is false, not only in the light of our faith, but in the light of the historical science to which that history has appealed.

2. Anti-Catholic history is most false and dangerous when it is not avowedly anti-Catholic.

3. Anti-Catholic history fails because history is a story; and it can never give the beginning of the story.

4. Anti-Catholic history is generally superficial; it depends on particular catchwords, cases and names, while Catholic history can handle the whole texture of the truth.

5. Anti-Catholic history is also helped by legend, which may be natural and even healthy, but is not scientific.

6. Anti-Catholic history constantly confesses an old error in launching a new one.

7. Anti-Catholic history is narrow and unimaginative, because it always conceives all men as looking forward to what did happen, instead of to the hundred things which might have happened or which most of them wished to happen.

8. Anti-Catholic history abounds in very casual remarks so false that they can only be contradicted by long and complicated statements.

9. Anti-Catholic history, in so far as it is Protestant, was a provincial misunderstanding of the high culture and even intellectual liberty of Catholicism.

10. Anti-Catholic history, in so far as it is atheistic or agnostic, has been a series of sweeping but very depressing scientific theories or generalizations, each applied rigorously to everything and each abandoned abruptly in favor of the next.

11. Anti-Catholic history, after bringing and dropping a thousand charges, after contradicting itself a thousand times, on the subject of the Catholic Church, has never yet guessed the simplest fact about that Church, that it stands for the whole truth against every kind of error.

12. Anti-Catholic history is obscurantist; it is afraid of the truth.

Granting that there may be lurking somewhere in Chesterton's indictment a trace of the *bête noire* in history—generalizations—there is nevertheless a fundamental truth in the lesson he conveys: "History must have a philosophy. It must tend to praise or to blame. It must judge. There is no such thing as mere external history, for all history is the history of the mind. Therefore, in anti-Catholic society history will be anti-Catholic. It will be anti-Catholic in the text-books. It will be anti-Catholic in examinations which Catholic youth has to pass. . . . The essentials of anti-Catholic history—the things which make it anti-Catholic—are first, the anti-Catholic *selection* of material; second, what is called the anti-Catholic *tone;* and third, the anti-Catholic *proportion* observed in the presentation of historical fact."

But to offset, or, as the scholastics might say, to distinguish this major premiss, it must be confessed quite honestly that the historian who writes on Catholic subjects without a complete knowledge of the same is most frequently unable to obtain a thoroughly critical interpretation of the facts from the standpoint of Catholic philosophy. There is, for example, a long litany of what may be called the historical objections against the Roman Catholic Church, the Catholic faith, the papacy, and Catholic political ideals. These objections are often badly handled by Catholic writers who approach them from the apologetic view-point, with the result that the non-Catholic student cannot escape the fear that an *a priori* method is being followed in their explanation or refutation.

There is only one scientific, and, therefore, legitimate, method to overcome the evil of pre-

judiced or ignorant anti-Catholic historical study
—and critical historians of non-Catholic faiths
deplore the evil as strongly as do Catholics—
and that is a renaissance of interest, of study, of
critical investigation of Catholicism's historical
past.   It is useless to complain about text-books,
when Catholic text-books of commanding historical merit are lacking.   It is useless to sit
by the waters of Babylon and mourn for the lost
Sion, if we hang our harps, silent, on the droop-
ing willow trees.   The Catholic Church is not
in exile anywhere in this world, and least of all
in English-speaking lands.   It is true that the
political temper of the times is to widen the
breach the Religious Rebellion of the sixteenth,
and the Revolution of the eighteenth, centuries,
effected between the Catholic Church and the
world of civilization and culture she moulded
and preserved.   But in no science can it be pro-
claimed with more surety that truth cannot
be   always   hidden,   than   in   the   historical
sciences.   *Magna est veritas et praevalebit.*

Hilaire Belloc's adventurous knight-errancy for
Catholic truth throbs with an enthusiasm which
is not shared by all his brethren in the faith; but
he is at his historic best when he writes: "The
fruition of the Catholic spirit led to an achievement, to a multitude and a magnitude in color,
in form, in device, in speculation, in the attain-

ing of intellectual and moral certitude, in law and in all social institutions, which we still precariously enjoy today. Here is the truth which must be rubbed in if we are to change the attitude of our opponent. Especially does primary education suffer everywhere from the anti-Catholic legend. Even they of the Faith, for the most part, take that legend for granted; especially in countries such as our own where the Catholic culture is known only to very few and where the Catholic tradition has been broken. The Catholics themselves in such circumstances boast of any special Catholic action in any field of learning as though it were an exception to be singled out. They accept the hostile interpretation of the Catholic past which is in the air around them. They measure contemporary national values by the false standards set them, conceiving, for instance, that Prussia is a success and Italy a failure. The task of reversing that anti-Catholic system is the hardest of all modern tasks. Yet must it be undertaken; for, although the most profound and the most active agent of change must always be spiritual action upon the individual, yet corporate action upon the mass is essential; and today *history* will act there as nothing else can do. In *history* we must abandon the defensive. We must carry the war into Africa.

We must make our opponents understand not only that they are wrong in their philosophy, not only ill-informed in their judgment of cause and effect, but out of touch with the past: which is ours."

Cardinal Newman has justly deplored the neglect of ecclesiastical history in his celebrated *Essay on Development.* "It is melancholy to say it," he writes, "but the chief, perhaps the only English writer who has any claim to be considered an ecclesiastical historian, is the unbeliever, Gibbon." The rapid changes which have come owing to history's ambition to make itself one of the exact sciences, have been particularly apparent in the domain of Church history, and many prominent names might be added to that of Gibbon, if indeed Gibbon has succeeded in preserving his fame as an historian. That there is a wider and deeper interest in ecclesiastical history is also proven by the numbers of historical reviews founded since 1880—*Revue d'Histoire Ecclésiastique* (Louvain), *Historisches Jahrbuch* (Munich), *Revue des Questions Historiques* (Paris), *Études* (Paris), *Bulletin d'Ancienne Littérature et d'Archéologie Chrétienne* (Paris), *Analecta Bollandiana* (Brussels), *Revue Bénédictine* (Maredsous), *Archivum Franciscanum Historicum* (Florence), *Revue Mabillon* (Paris),

*Nederlansch Archief voor Kerkgeschiedenis* ('s Gravenhage), the *Catholic Historical Review* (Washington), etc.

It cannot, however, be affirmed that ecclesiastical history has as yet been given the place of honor it deserves in our Catholic educational system and more especially in the theological training of our clergy. The second spring of a renaissance may not be far off, since there is all about us an awakening sense of the Catholic historical background to all the political problems disturbing the world today. It has been well said that Catholic education comes to its own in the study of Church history, and that "the Catholic mind is more at home among the phenomena and problems of history than other minds for whom the ages of faith are only vaults of superstitition or periods of mental servitude, or at best, ages of high romance." The Catholic mind understands better than any other the influence of the Church on the development of European history and thought during these later centuries.

Scarcely any more judicious summary of the value of Church history as a science of great intrinsic value to the priest and layman could be found than that contained in the essay on the *Teaching of Church History,* cited above. Taught on the broader and higher plateau of

man's origin and destiny, Church history is inval-
uable as a school of experience and judgment,
and one of the greatest teachers of truth.   Its
higher educational value can be summed up in
two main lines of thought:

I.   The study of Church history gives *great
principles* by which to judge of events past and
present.   Great principles, as Lacordaire says,
are like the granite rocks that support the universe; they are strong foundations hewn in the
immovable bedrock of time.   They stand the
test of time; they answer the questionings of
the ever-growing mind of the race; they serve as
a basis on which the edifice of a life's reading
may rise secure.   They are elementary, it is
true,—so elementary that they are on the first
page of our little Catechism, but they are indispensable to the right reading of history, and
hence of human progress, in any one of its five
phases—intellectual, industrial, social, political,
and religious.   In the light of these principles,
three results seem to follow:—

(a) *An admiration for the Church* that is full
of childlike love and loyalty.   She appears before
us not only as the mystic Bride of Christ, but as
the Mother and Mistress of the nations.   History shows her as the saviour of Europe, as when
at the time of the fall of the Roman Empire "the
Roman Primacy was the one fixed point in the

west while all else was fluctuating and transitional," and the Church, in the person of her Pontiff, went forth to face the invading hordes of barbarians, or when she roused Catholic princes to a realisation of the danger threatening Europe in the sixteenth century and brought about the defeat of the Turks at Lepanto. The Church is seen in history to be the great civilising power in the world, the great teacher and educator, the inspirer of true art and architecture and poetry, the protector and patron of learning. A study of the life history of her most illustrious Popes, of the work of religious Orders, and of the foundation and rise of European universities, reveals the Church as she really is. A right understanding of the lives of many of the Saints, and of what Europe owes to them, will increase this admiration for the Church, the inspirer and teacher of all true sanctity.

(b) *An assurance of mind that is undismayed, however grievous the accusations brought against the Church,* even should these accusations be true. We stand on such secure ground that what might be a scandal and stone of stumbling tends to strengthen faith rather than to undermine it. "The existence of the Church and the Papacy as they are today is a wonder only enhanced by every proof that they ought to have perished long ago according to all human probability." This assurance of mind brings with it the power of distinguishing with clearness between a great ideal and its realisation in actual life. Catholics should have an unperturbed conviction that the Church will have the last word in any controversy, and that she has nothing to be alarmed at, though all the battalions of newest thought should be set in array against her.

(c) The *possession of a clue to the right understanding of problems connected with the Church in the present day.* "How much ignorant, precipitate criticism of the Church's action would be avoided," says the excellent brochure we are following here, "if Catholics viewed contemporary events against a truer historical background. In late years this none too loyal spirit has revealed itself in the attitude of many minds towards such questions as Biblical Criticism and the decree *Ne Temere,* and the Concordat with France."

II. The study of European history gives *width of outlook and sympathy* that leads to cultivation of mind. "If such study opens out horizons to the mind, showing in perspective the stately processions of the centuries, each one indissolubly linked with the other, and points to the Church as giving the key to the whole, it widens too the power of sympathetic understanding of the past. Both mind and heart are richer for the accumulated treasures of the ages. History ceases to be a mere chronicle of past events and becomes a living, palpitating reality. Such a study, made in youth, lays the foundation of a life's interest. With the broad lines of history marked out, subsequent reading, instead of being desultory, is connected with former knowledge, sinking back into its true position in the mind, deepening thought and enriching experience. It causes persons and events to be judged, not in the light of the twentieth century, but by the standard of their own day; for events, no less than persons, cannot be taken out of their setting of century, country, and local coloring, without losing their true significance. The study of history makes every country seem like home. Travelling takes on a different aspect, while in places with a historic past, the streets, the buildings, the very atmosphere thrills with living interest. So life is richer for all that has been learned, and the whole world seems kin."

# CHAPTER IV

## THE STUDY OF CHURCH HISTORY

The ever-increasing literature on the modern scientific conception of historical study has placed considerable stress upon a threefold division of historiography, or the history of history writing. The logic of history has been busily at work for half a century endeavoring to find a substitute for the canonical divisions of history—ancient, medieval, and modern, owing to their misleading emphasis on the mind of the student. Writers on historiography, however, have on the contrary striven to classify all history writing or the concept of the functions of history under three heads —narrative, pragmatic, and genetic or scientific.

This classification is not so objectionable as the time-divisions, but it may become so quite easily unless the beginner is on his guard. Threefold divisions are a sort of fetish, and the student may unwittingly be led to conclude that all ancient historians are of the narrative kind; that all medieval and especially medieval Church historians are of the pragmatic or didactic kind;

and, with the exception of a few centuries while they were finding their way, that all modern historians are of the scientific or systematic kind.

The beginner is a beginner because he depends so largely on generalizations instead of detailed and accurate knowledge; and he will generalize by calling one historian a narrative writer, another, a didactic writer, and a third, a critical historical writer—the emphasis always being upon the lateness of the last in the field of historiography.

Unless he observes caution in his classifications, the student, as he puts down, for example, James Harvey Robinson's *New History,* will come to the conclusion that the "somewhat startling vicissitudes" of historical writing during the past twenty-five hundred years are not so startling after all, since the divisions are so easily made. The inference he will draw after reading the *New History* is that there are those who have followed the style of Herodotus, whom he will call the father of narrative history; those who have followed Thucydides, the father of history with a purpose; and those who today profit by the revolution von Ranke wrought in the historical sciences, namely, the modern scientific school of historians. There will be a confused idea in his mind how this last evolution came about; but in a vague way he will know that

Voltaire, Karl Marx, Darwin, and others, in some fashion influenced the change.

The difference between the narrative and didactic schools he will visualize as a distinction between an æsthetic and imaginative method of describing facts and that "deplorable" thing—the unfortunate use of history for political, moral or religious aims.   The distinction between the narrative and didactic style on the one hand and the systematic method on the other he will express to himself in radical terms—the historian's single aim should be the attainment of truth by the establishment of the facts, and his method must be solely to show how things came to be what they are, how things evolved from cause to effect—the *eigentlich geworden* ruling today in place of the *eigentlich gewesen* or *das Geschehene*.   This change in history from an amorphous branch of literature to a fully equipped science, with its own method, its canons of criticism, its auxiliary sciences, its own particular laws for the establishment of facts and for their coordination—this change is given almost a birthday with the founding of von Ranke's historical seminar at Berlin, in 1833.

Now all this is rather misleading.   Like all simple explanations in history, it invites suspicion in so complex a subject as the evolution of the historical sciences.   Ranke's seminar is indeed a point of departure in the history of history; but it is owing more to the great historian's personal influence on the original group he formed—Waitz, Jaffé, Giesebrecht, Sybel, Adolf Schmidt, Wattenbach, and others, that the *terminus a quo* of systematic history may be traced to him. These students, who all became renowned scholars in their particular fields, carried with them to other universities the seminar spirit and method; and their pupils in turn, brought von Ranke's system of historical training to other parts of the world. The inauguration, for example, of the courses in history under Herbert Baxter Adams, at Johns Hopkins University, in 1876, immediately after his return from the historical seminars of Göttingen, Berlin, and Heidelberg, is considered the beginning of modern historical scholarship in this country. Von Ranke died in 1886, and that date has become a sort of fixed star in the historical firmament as the beginning of the wide influence of his practical seminar system of historical training. Harry Elmer Barnes pays Ranke a merited tribute when he writes: "With the work of Ranke the foundations of modern historical scholarship were firmly laid. The progress since his time has consisted primarily in a further refinement of critical methods and their general dissemination among a continually growing body of historical scholars. This progressive expansion of scientific historical scholarship has been in part the result of the direct influence of von Ranke's methods by his students and in part the out-growth in every country of these same preliminary conditions and developments which made the work of von Ranke possible."

Under the stress, then, placed upon the development of history writing in general,—a stress which gives a chronological aspect to this development, the student of Church history may be led somewhat astray. Ecclesiastical historiography has not followed the same train of change and evolution as has history in general. In fact, a systematic treatise on the origins of the modern critical method would disclose the fact that practically speaking every influence which brought about the more wholesome use of a methodic approach to historical truth came from ecclesiastical historians who antedate von Ranke by one, two, or three centuries. Long ago, Langlois hinted in his *Manuel de Bibliographie Historique* (1904) that it is prudent not to emphasize the common opinion that critically written history dates from any definite epoch. Nor will he allow even the Renaissance to be taken as a point of departure. It is true that in all ages—as in our own—the critical sense is not widely distributed among students or scholars; but there has existed in every epoch a small group of exceptional minds, whose work shows the presence of the highest methodic values. The student of ecclesiastical historiography will have no difficulty in discovering, in every age of the Church, historians whose knowledge of historical research and of historical criticism must be given equal rank with that of the foremost scholars in the field today.

In all reverence to the inspired pages of St. Luke's *Acts of the Apostles*—the *Apostelgeschichte,* as the better German word has it—the student will find in this first little History of the Catholic Church a good example of many of the requirements for systematic history. We see the sources he used, and how he brings into his narrative his own personal experiences, his *former treatise,* the reminiscences of eye-witnesses to the events he relates (St. Paul, St. Peter, St. Mark, and St. Philip), and even the incorporation of public documents, as in chapter twenty-five. The purpose of the *Acts* was historical: to describe the development of the Church from the beginning down to the author's own day, which was sometime between 63 and 70 A. D. And what is noteworthy is that St. Luke does not claim that his narrative contains a complete history of the preaching of the Gospel up to that time.

A careful study of McGiffert's *Prolegomena* to

his translation of Eusebius' *Church History* will leave no doubt in the beginner's mind that in the Father of Ecclesiastical History modern systematic or critical history has an actual founder, despite the fact that fifteen centuries separate this first historian of the Church from Ranke's day. McGiffert writes: "The whole Christian world has reason to be thankful that there lived at the opening of the fourth century a man who, with his life spanning one of the greatest epochs that has occurred in the history of the Church, with an intimate experimental knowledge of the old and of the new condition of things, was able to conceive so grand a plan and possessed the means and the ability to carry it out. Had he written nothing else, Eusebius' *Church History* would have made him immortal; for if immortality be a fitting reward for large and lasting services, few possess a clearer title to it than the author of that work." The wealth of the documentary material Eusebius uses in his *Church History,* the precious citations he makes from writers before his time, and the untold value of his own commentary on contemporary events in solving many of the historical problems of the early Church which otherwise would remain riddles to us; the extensive personal knowledge he possessed, and his generous incorporation of many historical works now lost to us—all these factors bring Eusebius very near to the moderns, who exact of the historian scholarly accuracy combined with vast learning. Eusebius has defects, serious defects, as Shotwell has described them in his *Introduction to the History of History,* and the chief of these is not alone his woeful lack of literary style. This is one of the more noticeable faults in his work. McGiffert calls it: "His complete lack of any conception of historiography as a fine art." But measured by our strictest modern canons of criticism, Eusebius displays everywhere the marks of the genuine historical spirit. His diligent use of his source-material, the wide range of his research, his marvellous sagacity in the selection of documents, and his great wisdom in the discriminating way he has of contrasting reliable and unreliable material—these are his claims to preëminence in critical ecclesiastical history. He is constantly sincere; unfailingly honest. One of the decisive signs of his veracity is "the frankness with which he confesses his lack of knowledge upon any subject and the care with which he distinguishes the different kinds of evidence upon which he bases his statements."

It is well, then, for the student of Church history who may be influenced by the opinion that our modern methods are the *discovery* of the German historical seminar system, to realize that

out of the pages of Bishop Eusebius' *Chronicle,
Church History,* and *Life of Constantine*—to
mention only his principal works—might be
drawn a group of splendid critical rules which he
practiced. The *plan of the whole* which opens
the first chapter of the *Church History* ought to
be memorized by every student. This does not
mean that the beginner has no obligation to master at least one good text-book on the Historical
Method. What he needs to be warned against
is being led astray by the inference that critical
ecclesiastical history is a result—as general history may be considered—of the Humanistic
movement. The very dates of the manuals on
methodology are provocative of such a misleading conclusion.

In 1889, the first edition of that *meisterwerk,*
Ernest Bernheim's *Lehrbuch der historischen
Methode,* appeared at Leipzig, and the scientific
historical world had at last a standard treatise
upon which practically all the books on the subject have since been based. Chief among these
is the *Introduction to the Study of History* by
MM. Langlois and Seignobos, first published in
1897; an English translation (by G. G. Berry)
appeared in London, in 1898. Professor F. M.
Fling published a valuable synthesis of Bernheim's work—*Outline of Historical Method,* in
1899. Many other volumes on the method have

since been printed. Among these may be cited: J. M. Vincent's *Historical Research: an Outline of Theory and Practice* (1911). From Catholic authors came many similar works: Battaini, *Manuale di Metodologia Storica* (1904); Fonck, *Wissenschaftliches Arbeiten* (1908), translated as *Le Travail Scientifique* (1911); Albers, *Manuale di Propædutica Storica* (1909); and what is without doubt the most excellent treatise on the subject, Feder's *Lehrbuch der geschichtlichen Methode,* the third revised and enlarged edition of which was printed in 1924. Recently (1921), the second edition of that excellent manual, *Metodologia y Critica historicas* by Villada, appeared at Barcelona.

The student will also find the two following works of value in directing him towards the mastery of the larger works: Meister's *Grundzüge der historischen Methode* (1913, 65 pp.), and Brehier-DuDezert, *Le Travail Historique* (1914, 52 pp.). The latter volume is no. 426 of the collection *Science et Religion.* The series *Helps for Students* (S. P. C. K.) contains three short treatises: Crump, *The Logic of History* (61 pp.), Johnson, *The Mechanical Processes of the Historian* (30 pp.), and Marshall, *The Historical Criticism of Documents* (62 pp.). All these volumes contain bibliographical indications for the literature on the subject of method.

Bernheim published in 1905 a synopsis of his great work under the title, *Einleitung in die Geschichtswissenschaft*. A *Bibliography of the Study and Teaching of History* will be found in the *Annual Report* of the American Historical Association (1899), by James I. Wyer; and his list will be found brought up to date (1916) in Henry Johnson's admirably written volume, *The Teaching of History*. Fling's latest (1920) treatise: *The Writing of History—an Introduction to Historical Method* is marred by a spirit closely approaching the anti-Christian.

The Catholic student does not need to be reminded that the citation of these volumes is not an endorsement of all their contents and still less an approval of their philosophical tenor. Those by non-Catholic authors are frankly incredulous and skeptical and teach the complete divorce of systematic history from religion, ethics, or political theories.

The application of all this development in methodic analysis and synthesis to the study of ecclesiastical history has produced the following works, among many. De Smedt's *Introductio Generalis ad Historiam Ecclesiasticam critice Tractandam* (1876), is a guide to ecclesiastical documents. His celebrated treatise *Principes de la Critique Historique* is the first synthesis of the scientific basis for the work of the Bollandists, begun in 1615. Nirschl's *Propädeutik der Kirchengeschichte* (1898), Besse, *Les Études Historiques d'après la Méthode de Mabillon* (1900), and Kihn's *Encyclopädie und Methodologie der Theologie* (*Kirchengeschichte* at pp. 289–383), published in 1892, are excellent service books for the student of Church history. A good manual (pp. 163), is De Schepper, *Inleiding tot de Studie der Kerkgeschiedenis,* published at Bruges, 1915. Acquoy's *Handleiding tot de Kerkgeschiedvorsching en Kerkgeschiedschrijving* (1894) contains a systematic bibliography of Church history. The student who can read Latin will find in the third (1916) edition of Benigni's *Historiæ Ecclesiasticæ Propaedeutica* all that he needs by way of initiation into the subject. The student of Catholic Church history will find little direction for his study in Baur, *Epochen der kirchlichen Geschichtschreibung* (Tübingen, 1852).

Let us admit at once that the difference between the student who must remain an *amateur* in Church history and the student who will be able to enrich scholarship lies basically in the most elementary of his *instruments de travail*—the languages. Without a thorough knowledge of classical and patristic Greek and Latin, the period of Christian antiquity can only be studied superficially; without a knowledge of medieval Latin—the *media latinitas* from which the Middle Ages probably received their name—his study of the second period of Church history will never rise above that of the dilettante; without at least a reading knowledge of the modern tongues—German, French, Italian, Spanish, English, and Polish (and in this order of importance), it is idle for the student of ecclesiastical history to hope for "new stars" in his journey towards scholarship. In proportion, therefore, as his knowledge of these is limited, so also must the circle of his ambitions be drawn closer. His knowledge of Latin, especially of Church Latin, will aid him for the medieval epoch, but unless he knows German thoroughly, many avenues of research must be permanently closed to him.

It would be of the highest value to the student if the great Church historians from Eusebius to von Pastor had all described in detail the causes motivating their love for Church history and the rules of method they evolved for themselves in its study. Here and there in their pages, in prefaces and in introductions, and at difficult moments in the development of their narrative, critical judgments on the value of their source-material and on the particular critical analysis which helped them to establish the authenticity of a document or of a fact will escape their pens. But these are scarcely more than glimpses into their workshop. There are exceptions: St.

Bede in the eighth century; Baronius in the sixteenth; Bossuet, Tillemont and Mabillon in the
seventeenth; Fleury, Natalis Alexander, Charles
Dodd, Cardinal Orsi, Bishop Walmesley, and
others, in the eighteenth; Milner, J. A. Möhler,
Lanigan, Lingard, Cardinal Mai, Rohrbacher,
Cardinal Newman, Cardinal Hergenröther, Janssen, Hefele, de Rossi, Jungmann, and others in
the nineteenth century; and the Church historians
whose works are preëminent for critical scholarship in our own days—Duchesne, Pastor, Cardinal Gasquet, Batiffol, Denifle, Alfred Cauchie,
and many others. Out of their learned historical
productions, the future ecclesiastical historio-
grapher will one day be able to deduce, as Dom
Besse has done with Mabillon, the fruits of their
personal experiences and the sources for their
success.

If we search their volumes for the purpose of
ascertaining how the study of Church history
should be pursued by the young scholar, a definite
method of approach can be established. Collins
sums up the problem in his chapter on *How to
Study Ecclesiastical History*. He is not, be it
understood, dealing with the specialist, that is
with the student who has reached a certain
amount of proficiency in the work of analysis
and synthesis, nor with the general reader of
Church history, but with the neophyte who de-

sires to prepare himself for the technical formation necessary to specialized critical work in the
field.   Collins looks at the problem from a practical standpoint, and decides that there are two
ways of setting to work on the study of ecclesiastical history.   "On the one hand, the student
might make it his endeavor to get into his head
*a general idea of the history of the Christian
Church from its beginning to the present day,* and
then gradually deepen and widen his knowledge,
passing by degrees to the detailed investigation
of particular subjects.   He might, for instance,
*begin with a short text-book,* and then go on to
a longer one, and then to one of the general
Church histories, and then to the histories of
special periods, to the monographs on particular
points, and so on.   Or *he might begin at exactly
the opposite end.*   He might take, for example,
some *well-written biography of a great man,* or
some clear and straightforward *history of an important crisis* or *interesting period,* and use this
as a starting point, deepening his knowledge as
he goes on, and stretching out from this as a
centre on both hands, seeking light from the
events that went before and that followed after,
and bringing to them the reflected light from his
own period.   In a word, he might either work
from *the general to the particular,* or from *the
particular to the general.*   Now which of these

is the better way of setting to work? Perhaps
our first impulse might be to say that *the former
is the better way;* and certainly it is that which
most would-be students incline to adopt. Nevertheless, it seems clear that this is not really the
most natural order of procedure, nor is it the
best. The *experimental method* which we have
used since we were babes undoubtedly began with
the investigation of details; and it would be a
very surprising thing if, in such a science as history, *the best method of study* were one that proceeded *from generals to particulars.* We cannot
do anything without having a definite base; we
cannot exert any power without a fulcrum; we
cannot even draw a straight line without starting
from a point. Again, even if it were desirable
in other ways to attempt it, it would not really
be possible to obtain a general view of Church
history, so as to work by the deductive method;
for we must never forget that the history of the
Church is not finished. And once more, on the
practical side, such a method would be doomed
to failure by its dulness; for in history as in life,
we cannot get away from the details without losing much of our interest and much of our grasp
of truth. *From every point of view, then, the
right method of study is that which begins by
taking some definite subject for investigation.*"

This procedure means in reality the creation of

a "hobby," that is, some special subject for study. Providing there is sufficient interest at the outset, it matters little what the subject is. If it be found uninteresting after a reasonable amount of reading, it will lead to another. Anything the student takes up and really studies, says Collins, "is sure to prove worthy of study, for the real way to find any subject in God's world interesting is to take an interest in it. It will form a kind of centre for his reading and his thoughts; for he is sure to find his thoughts turning towards it refreshingly. . . . And he will find that this method of study has another advantage. The ordinary parish priest is apt to say that he has no time to read. Such a state of things would be grievous indeed; for unless there be time to pray and to study, all else must go wrong; and the time which is snatched from reading and prayer is simply squandered. But it is not quite true that he has no time to read. The parish priest has a good deal of time on his hands, but it is mostly broken up into very short periods, or else it comes when he is very tired; and he is always liable to be interrupted. Under these circumstances it is very hard indeed to get much reading done, unless there is some definite object in view. No man can start upon some new work when he is tired out; no man can do much at it in odd periods of five minutes. But with such a 'hobby' as has been described, things are different. It is possible to follow up a scent even when we are tired out; it is possible to work at a subject in which we are keenly interested even for odd periods of five minutes. Some of John Richard Green's best historical work was done when he was curate-in-charge of an East End parish; and there are those yet living there who can tell us that he in no way neglected the duties of his charge. So also, much of the fifth volume of Bishop Creighton's *History of the Papacy* was written in odd periods of a few minutes, in the intervals between appointments, or as he travelled about his diocese."

To these examples from the Anglican Church, the Catholic student may add many of equal merit. On the memorial tablet over the Venerable Bede's tomb at Durham, one reads: "An Englishman born in an obscure corner of the world, he, by his knowledge enlightened the whole universe, for he searched the treasury of divine and human learning." Yet the forty years of his study and writing were spent in his monastery at Jarrow, uninterrupted by absence or travel. He was ordained at the age of thirty, and the next thirty years were spent in all the varied duties of his monastic life, in preaching and in teaching— he is indeed considered the father of English elementary education.

lege. In 1811, he accepted the parish at Hornby, about eight miles from Lancaster. Here he produced his celebrated *History of England*. Eleven years of preparatory work antedated the appearance of the first three volumes in 1819, and the tenth was published in 1830. The student who reads the *Life of Lingard* by Haile-Bonney (1912) will find many interesting letters from Dr. Lingard's pen on the question of how best to present the truth of Catholic history to non-Catholic readers. During all these years at Hornby, he neglected none of his priestly duties. Lingard left behind him thirty-two historical productions.

Father Johannes Janssen (1829–1891) had a better scholastic and university training than Lingard. He had studied at Louvain, under Laforet and Moeller; at Bonn, under Aschbach and Dahlmann; and won his doctorate at Bonn in 1853. As a teacher in Frankfort his interests were directed by Johann Frederick Böhmer to the study of the German people. Eight volumes of his *History of the German People* were published —six by Janssen himself (1876–88), and two by his friend and disciple, the celebrated historian of the Popes, Ludwig von Pastor (1893–94). Pastor's charming *Lebensbild* of Janssen (1894) tells the story of his devotion to all the spiritual works which came within his round of duties.

The literary and critical merits of his *History* place Janssen among the foremost Catholic historians of the last century. He escaped more than one bishopric, and declined to accept the cardinalate. He is remembered for his devotion to the poor and the sick, and he gave liberally from his means to all works of mercy. Frankfort has today an asylum for abandoned children which was built mainly through his efforts and generosity.

With examples such as these before us, it will not be unfair to conclude that once a centre of interest has been created, the idea that will be formed will awaken all the powers of the mind and heart. Collins warns those for whom he writes—his fellow-Anglican clergy—that "even a slight examination of the field of ecclesiastical history may easily involve a considerable amount of reading, extending over a very wide range. This is inevitable and unavoidable: from the very nature of his work the student of history has to make use of more books than almost any other student."

It sometimes happens, in consequence, that the beginner is discouraged not only by the tax he places upon his memory, but by the facile way the apparent results of his study and reading escape him. "The more faithfully and impartially he sets about his work, the more likely is the student to experience a certain feeling of dissatisfaction with the results.    It is not simply that he will be painfully conscious of the imperfections of his own work . . . but the conclusions to which his study of the evidence lead him are likely to disappoint him." Again, "many who enter upon the study of ecclesiastical history with avidity make no real headway because after a time they get discouraged.    They seem to make quick progress at first, and everything looks simple enough; but after a time they discover that the progress has slackened, and that the same amount of labor expended does not produce anything like the same apparent result.    They therefore begin looking elsewhere, in the hope of finding some employment in which they can hope for quicker and more abundant returns.    It is not surprising, however, that the results should seem to be less as the work proceeds; all that it means is that the *law of diminishing returns* applies to ecclesiastical history as it applies to everything else.    We do not expect to find that a double expenditure of fuel will double the speed of our warships, or that a double charge of powder will send a projectile twice as far as the single charge; nor can we reasonably expect to find it otherwise with regard to the study of ecclesiastical history. At any rate, the law does so apply, both in this and in every other scientific study. He who would do any real work must be prepared to recognise the fact, to face much drudgery for which he will never have anything to show, and to apply himself all the more diligently because the results seem few and far between. He will have his reward; not perhaps that of which he dreamed at first, but one far better worth the winning."

It is not easy to answer the question of discouragement. Sometimes it is due to a want of a methodic and logical plan of work; sometimes, to the mistake of abandoning such a plan; but more often it is the result of a lack of recognition of one's own limitations. Presupposing that the student has read at least one good Manual of Church history, he must accept the first law of the higher learning—the law of limitations. In historical study, limitation is secured by one of three ways: *time, place,* or *idea;* that is, he will place chronological or geographical limits to his choice for study, or he will take up one special aspect of Church history, endeavor to obtain a general view of its rise and development, and then limit his real work to a certain period or a certain nation or place. Excluding profane (political, social, economic, literary, etc.) history, these special categories are so many that it would be impracticable to list them. The following topics, given without any basic order, may suggest an approach to these subject limitations:

1. *History of the Popes*—chief events of their lives; their official messages to the Church at large, etc.

2. *History of Church government*—the constitution of the Church; pontifical authority; the hierarchy; disciplinary decrees; canon law; ecclesiastical jurisdiction; benefices; church property rights; customs in local churches; Christian folklore, etc.

3. *History of Christian worship*—liturgy; various rites and ceremonies; history of holydays of obligation; the history of the Sacraments; history of the Mass, the Divine Office, the *Ritual;* history of the Blessed Sacrament; Forty Hours' Devotion; construction of churches, their art and architecture; superstitions, etc.

4. *History of the propagation of the Church* —the preaching of the Gospel; methods of conversion; history of homiletics; miracles; establishment of episcopal sees; the history of noted converts; psychology of conversion, etc.

5. *History of the victories of the Church*—persecutions; martyrs, etc.

6. *History of rebellions against the authority of the Church*—apostates; heretics; schismatics; rise of non-Catholic Christian sects, etc.

7. *History of the Councils.*
8. *History of celebrated churchmen.*
9. *History of ecclesiastical writers*—Fathers and Doctors of the Church; theologians, philosophers, etc. etc.
10. *History of the Saints*—by periods; by nations; by religious orders; laymen and laywomen; children saints etc. etc.
11. *History of canonization.*
12. *History of theological controversies in the Church.*
13. *History of the Religious Orders.*

Once the student has found the particular field which interests him, it is prudent for him to learn thoroughly one general work on his special subject before beginning to study the more special detail he intends to master. For example, the general history of the Religious Orders might first be read in Heimbucher's *Die Orden and Kongregationen der Katholischen Kirche* (second revised and greatly enlarged edition, Paderborn, 1907–08). Here the student will find the amplest bibliographical directions for any particular Order or Congregation or for any particular phase of its activity. Scannell in his *Priest's Studies* gives a number of suggestions regarding specialization. He recommends to the clergy to study first of all the Church history of their own country, and from this local or national centre to proceed to the more general field. A further

suggestion is to take up the life of some leading
character in the Church and study him in his environment.   For example, the history of Arianism
can be studied by following the life of St. Athan-
asius.   The figure of Pope Leo I (457–474)
will stand out in the fifth century, and around
him can be centred the general story of the
Church and the barbarian world.   The life of
Pope Gregory the Great (590–604) will serve as
a central focus for the monasteries and the
progress of monasticism.   The life of Charlemagne can be made the avenue to a detailed study
of the rise of the Papal States.   The life of
Gregory VII (1073–1085) can well be made the
focus of the struggle between the Empire and the
Papacy.   The life of Innocent III (1198–1216)
will give the student a profound knowledge of the
Papacy and of the more attractive side of international life in the Middle Ages.   The life of
St. Thomas Aquinas, as for example the one by
Vaughan, Drane's *Christian Schools and Scholars,*
of which a new edition has recently been published,
and James J. Walsh's encyclopedic work, *The
Thirteenth the Greatest of Centuries,* will initiate
the student roughly into the age of the grandeur
of Catholic thought and life.   Salembier's *Great
Western Schism* will be a fitting prelude to
a study of the Reformation, and Baudrillart's
*Catholic Church, the Renaissance and Protes-*

*tantism* will explain the causes of the leading intellectual and politico-religious movements of the sixteenth century. Gasquet's *Eve of the Reformation* and his *Henry VIII and the English Monasteries* will prepare the way for a detailed study of Protestantism in the British Isles. The bibliographies at the head of the chapters of Mac-Caffrey's *History of the Catholic Church in the Nineteenth Century* indicate some sources for the modern period.

Besides individual persons of prominence in Church history, the history of cities where the Church has been the foremost factor at certain periods, should be studied. Frederick Harrison's book, *The Meaning of History,* contains chapters on Rome, Constantinople, Paris, and London.

A simple method for the beginner in his choice of books for a particular study is to imagine the whole literature on or about his subject divided into three principal classes—*repertories, didactic books*, and *periodicals.*

(a) By *repertories* is meant any book that sets out deliberately to guide the searcher, as, for example, dictionaries of persons, dictionaries of historical events, biographical lists, guides, bibliographical lists, and encyclopedias.

(b) By *didactic books* are meant all historical works on the general aspect of the student's special topic, upon the topic itself, and on all aspects of that topic.

(c) By *periodicals* are meant solely those periodicals which are published in the student's particular field, namely, historical reviews.

Suppose then, that the student, already familiar with general Church history, should come upon that long list of the principal difficulties in ecclesiastical history which Mabillon drew up in the seventeenth century and which is printed at the end of Dom Besse's volume, or upon the list of special topics suggested in Abbé Blanc's four volumes, *Cours d'Histoire Ecclésiastique,* and should decide to take up for special study the *Suppression of the Templars.*

1. He might begin by opening the sixteenth volume or Index to the *Catholic Encyclopedia.* At the word *Templars,* he will find forty-four references to the volumes of that work. Each of these references should be put on a separate card with the mnemonic, *e. g.,* CE, IV–21c:— *Suppression.* One by one each of these *loci* are read and from each two sets of cards—*fiches* as the French students call them—are made: *one for facts* and *one for bibliographical references.* On each of these the exact volume and page of the *Catholic Encyclopedia* will be put, so that at any moment the student will be able to trace the source for the same. The result of this first in-

vestigation will be: (a) *a rudimentary knowledge*
of the Knights Templars, of their origin and
activities, and of the causes alleged for their
suppression; (b) *a list of references* on the subject, ranging from source-collections, general
works, lives of the Popes who reigned during the
trial and afterwards, of the principal Templars
involved in the fall of the Order, references to
national histories containing the story of the
trials in those countries, histories of the general
Council of Vienne (1311–12), histories of the
Avignon period of the Papacy, and references to
articles in reviews and historical periodicals.

2. The second stage of researches includes
the broadening and the deepening of the student's
knowledge of the Templars and of all the causes
brought forward for their suppression. This
the student will be able to acquire by a systematic
or logical reading of the didactic works in
his bibliographical list. Time may be saved
if advice be asked of a scholar who is recognised
as an authority in the field or in the period of their
suppression (1307–1312). In this way the student will give his first attention to the best book
on the subject, and from this book as a base he
will be able to go out into the source-material contained in other didactic books or in collections of
sources. At each step of the way, he will keep
on with the work of adding to his cards, one set

being for *facts,* and the other for *bibliographical references*. When he feels that he has made sufficient progress in his subject, it is wise to complete the bibliographical work with a quick research of the third division we have given. For various systems in the handling of card indexes (*fiches*) the student can find no better guide than Dow's *Principles of a Note-System for Historical Studies* (1924).

3. Historical periodicals. These are many and so a choice should be made. Perhaps the best of them for this particular subject is the *Revue d'Histoire Ecclésiastique* of Louvain, which chronicles the latest pertinent literature.

By the time all this preliminary research has been done the student finds that *pari passu* he has acquired a good knowledge of the origin, growth, and fall of the Knights Templars, as well as a clear insight into the times in which this great military order existed (1118–1312). If he is further inclined to make a critical study of the sources he has seen, an interesting problem presents itself: namely, how the Templars have fared at the hands of historians. He sees that their suppression is condemned by Mosheim, Voltaire, and by many authors who have been influenced by the desire to charge the Popes with blunders. For the affirmative he will find Natalis Alexander, Palma, Moeller, and many others.

It is a problem still discussed by scholars, and will continue to be, until historians are certain that all the documents on the suppression have been sifted.

A rather ingenious, albeit practical, treatise of how to study ecclesiastical history is given in Blanc's *Introduction*. Blanc distinguishes three classes of persons and three methods of degrees corresponding to these classes in the study of Church history. The *first class*—that of the simple faithful, sufficiently instructed to read Church history with intelligence and profit—approaches the subject for the purpose of further instruction and for edification. Wishing to know more about the faith they profess and to learn from the examples of Catholics in ages that are past how to practise their faith better, these need nothing more than a short history of the Church which will give them a general view but which will emphasize the great personages of Church history whose lives are filled with the sweetness and light of Christian virtue. They should then turn to a worthy volume or series of volumes on the lives of the Saints, such as Alban Butler's celebrated work, and confine their reading to this class of historical writing. Some of the volumes in the series *Les Saints* have been translated into English. It would be useless to multiply citations, since this first class will need to be directed by those who are familiar with elementary historical literature. Perhaps the best of this class of books is the *Quarterly Series,* edited by the Jesuit Fathers, of London. There is also a series called the *Friar Saints* and another called the *St. Nicholas Series,* written for the general reader, both of which deserve mention in this connection.

The *second class,* really the first deserving the name of historical students, consists of all those who have sufficient knowledge of the political history of the past and of Church history in general to begin a more detailed line of work. To these, Abbé Blanc recommends a serious study on the following plan: a review of the state of the world before the coming of Christ; a thorough knowledge of the history of the Jews; a brief survey of the history of the Old and New Testaments; the mastery of one good volume on the Roman Empire to the year 300, and then a careful reading of a general history of the Church, such as Rohrbacher, Alzog, Hergenröther, or Mourret. After this is finished, each period should be taken up separately and studied in such volumes as those included in the *Bibliothèque de l'Enseignement de l'Histoire Ecclésiastique* (Paris, Gabalda). If the student is in doubt which period to make his special field, Blanc recommends the first six centuries as meriting his principal attention.   Side-by-side with all this reading, should go a study of the political and social conditions of the times.

With the *third class,* namely with those students who look to scholarship in the field of Church history and therefore to a life consecration to its study, two methods are suggested—the one purely historical, the other, philosophical.

The first will carry the student beyond all that has been written in a discursive or detailed fashion to the sources, whether printed or unprinted, literary or monumental, with the purpose of investigating these sources either to ascertain new facts, new hypotheses for facts, new syntheses of facts, or new conclusions based on facts already known.   The object of this profound application to the science is to penetrate into the knowledge of the past by discoveries of an historical, literary, or archeological nature.

The second method, that of the philosophy of Church history, will demand as a preliminary condition a complete, thorough, and highly developed historical knowledge of the past, before the work of seeking out the laws which have reigned in the evolution of that past be ascertained and weighed.   Few will reach this realm of the stars.   St. Augustine and Bossuet—and to some extent Balmes—remain alone in their glory as the only authors who have successfully treated Church history upon the basis of Christian philosophy. Very few works exist on the subject of the Catholic philosophy of history; perhaps, the only two worthy of mention, besides Schlegel's *Philosophy of History* and Allies' *Formation of Christendom,* are Cathrein's *Die Katholische Weltanschauung in ihren Grundlinien,* a second edition of which appeared in 1909, and F. Sawicki's *Geschichtsphilosophie,* in the *Philosophische Handbibliothek* (Munich, 1920). And it is difficult to define the idea contained in the term itself.

To reach the sublime heights of a Catholic philosophy of history, the scholar must transcend simple facts and series of facts and, viewing the whole story of the Church's progress through the ages, reach out to find the fundamental laws which have governed its development. He must be able to recognize and to observe the special guardianship of Divine Providence over the Spouse of Christ, the ravishing harmony which binds together all parts of the City of God on earth, and formulate for the explanation of the divine life within the Church, answers to those problems which have ever vexed the hearts of men—what is the origin of humanity; what is its final end; and what are the general and permanent factors which guide humanity towards its final end? Here the historian touches science at every part of the vast circumference which surrounds our knowledge of man and nature. St. Paul gave the answer nineteen hundred years ago, when standing before the Athenians in the Areopagus: "God, who made the world and all things therein . . . and hath made of one, all mankind, to dwell upon the whole face of the earth, determining appointed times and the limits of their habitation. That they should seek God, if haply they may feel after him or find him, although he be not far from every one of us. For in him we live and move and are. . . . Because he hath appointed a day wherein he will judge the world in equity, by the man whom he hath appointed: giving faith to all, by raising him up from the dead." In these profound terms St. Paul gives the divine plan for the existence of creation and for the development of humanity, together with the cardinal points and the permanent factors that intervene in its progress towards eternity.

It is because of this lofty possibility in the study of the Church of God that the student should come to his task with sentiments of the highest devotion. The Church whose life he wishes to know is the Mother of the great Christian family, the sons and daughters of which from the days of the Apostles to our own no man may number. The Church is the *patria* of the Christian, the terrestrial *patria,* to live in which as a citizen is a foretaste of the eternal home towards which his heart ever sends out longing anticipations. The first requisite, therefore, in the student of Church history, is love for the Church, that love which the Latins knew best how to name when they called it *pietas*. With this filial piety towards the Church goes hand-in-hand zeal—zeal for truth and zeal for justice; not a zeal which outruns prudence in dealing with difficult or unhappy periods in the history of the Church, but an enlightened zeal which measures the whole course of the Church's combats, her successes and her failures, in the divine light of her constitution, her members, and her destiny. The second requisite is love for the truth. Veracity is the fundamental law of history; and since ecclesiastical history treats of things that are above the natural order, the spirit of truthfulness rises so much the higher and demands all the stronger allegiance.

The Church has no need of lies to face the world in any discussion of her past. Even a slight acquaintance with modern literature will convince the student that in the question of veracity he is at a serious disadvantage when face to face with many non-Catholic historians, who weave their narrative so skilfully "that, without straying from the truth, the history of the Church may be made to appear a chronicle of scandals." The Church, as Devas says in his *Key to the World's Progress,* must pay the penalty for her title of Catholic, since "she is formed of a miscellaneous crowd that nature would speedily scatter and that grace alone unites." The Church is not and never has been a congregation of the perfect, but a training school for the imperfect; and the Catholic student of her history must hold fast to the fact that "to mistake the Church Militant for the Church Triumphant is an heretical anachronism." Her history is the mirror of the history of her divine Founder, to whom she is joined in the mystic bonds of love as His Spouse.

"If these things are so, how all important is a true delineation of the Church, how enkindled should be every ambition to achieve so incomparable an end! It was worth while when the Roman Empire stretched over Western Europe and Northern Africa and hither Asia, to attempt the history of so magnificent a growth. It was worth while again when the British Empire within the brief span of some hundred years had arisen and spread over the earth, to attempt the history of such a progress, and trace the humble sources of so mighty a stream. Still more was it worth while in the days of Eusebius of Cæsarea, though

he might shrink from the task as too great for his
strength, to gather up into one body the scattered
records of the Church, to set forth her glories,
and to answer the pagan reproach that she was
but a thing of yesterday, by showing her foundations to have been laid with the foundations of
the world.   And now, after the further lapse of
nearly sixteen centuries, how much more is it
worth while to set forth the annals of the faith,
to tell the lengthened tale of heroism, to discern
the home of grace and sanctity, to display man in
his true manhood, and our reason sustained
against the persistent attacks of ever-varying un-
reason, to recognise the undying torch-bearer, dis-
sipating the obscurity of our mortal life till the
time of darkness is over, as she goes forth, faithful and true, to meet the immortal Bridegroom
with whose heart she has ever been in sweet accord (*cor ad cor loquitur*) and to pass into all
truth and never-fading light (*ex umbris et ima-
ginibus in veritatem*).   Lovers gaze gladly on
the likeness of one they love; and gladly therefore should we gaze on the authentic portrait of
the Church, and dwell lovingly on the features of
the never-failing friend of all the sons of men: this
Church who by her very nature is the loving
mother of us all; the mother of those whose fresh
youth is not yet dimmed by sophistry, nor made
crafty by deception, nor soured by disappoint-

ment, nor hardened by iniquity; the mother who may be thrust aside in the hour of prosperity, but is the ever ready refuge, to whom those can turn whose burdens are heavy, whose hopes are shattered, whose days are drawing to a close, whose hearts are aching with irremediable sorrow. Ah! indeed in this dark world of illusion it is worth while to make her known; for to know her is to love her."

# CHAPTER V

## THE FORMATION OF THE ECCLESIASTICAL HISTORIAN

The formation of the ecclesiastical historian consists of three stages or steps which may be described as: 1. a general knowledge of Church history; 2. a knowledge of the principles of historical method; and 3. the practical application of these principles to a well-chosen subject from the general field of ecclesiastical history.

The knowledge of Church history in general is the basic element or foundation of historical scholarship. That scholarship becomes a possibility when the student has progressed far enough in his reading to warrant his choice of a special subject for detailed study. Upon this self-imposed limitation, either by time, place, or idea, rests the real formation of the scholar. Scholarship will begin when the student believes that in the historical science lies his intellectual consecration. A vocation consists mainly of two elements —desire and adaptability. The student's desire to make Church history his choice field of intel-

lectual activity springs from hidden impulses
which even he himself may be unable to explain.
Such a desire is an interior illumination of the
spirit. The tangible parts of the consecration
itself are many; chief amongst these are honesty
of purpose, sincerity of aim, and affection for his
subject. Desire alone, even when linked with an
aptitude or talent for the work, will not create
the scholarship demanded today of the historian.
"Ability without method," says Bernheim, "is as
detrimental to science as method without ability."
And in no science is this so true as in history.
The very nature of history makes it a popular field
for study. Waitz says somewhere: "Perhaps no
science has more to suffer from dilettantism than
history."

Without a methodic training in the science
of history, the student must remain an *amateur*—
and *amateurs* have been the bane of Church
history since the Church began. The mere
knowledge, however, of the scientific method of
reasoning will not lead to right conclusions any
more than "the mere possession of a chest of
tools will make a man a carpenter; . . . but with
equal natural ability, equal study, and equal experience, the man who is provided with a good
method will outstrip him who employs a defective
or feeble method or who trusts to mere common
sense."

Hence the necessity of the student finding out for himself by means of mastering the method step by step whether he possesses the adaptability for the study of Church history. The adaptability requisite for a whole-hearted consecration to any kind of work is threefold—physical, moral, and intellectual. Here it is question of the two latter only, though the first can not be excluded. Many a student of the medieval and early modern periods of Church history has suffered permanently from long hours spent over almost indecipherable documents, or documents glistening with the sand that still remains on them. To the glory of American letters there stands forever the superb moral heroism of a great historian who overcame the physical weakness caused by so much study and reading—Francis Parkman. No student can read the story of Parkman's wooden frame with its horizontal wires to guide his hand in writing and not be moved by such an example of fortitude. "For the first half year," Parkman tells us, "the rate of composition averaged about six lines a day."

The moral ability necessary for perfection in historical science can not be assumed. Like all virtue it must be fought for, and when won, fought for again. All the flaws in historical study proceed from the absence of the virtues proper to the science. Reason, or intellect, is not absolute or independent in man. It must be developed by intellectual and moral virtues, the chief of which are prudence, justice, temperance, and fortitude. Of these the two which are necessary for the student's progress in historical science are justice and prudence. Justice rules over the historian's sense of veracity. Prudence is the queen of all virtues. The intellect is so often blinded or led astray—consciously or unconsciously—by passion, interest, desire, fear, or other tendencies leading to partiality, that it no longer discerns the golden rule of strict justice, temperance, or fortitude. "Thus, without prudence, fortitude passes into rashness, vindictive justice into harshness, clemency into weakness, religion into superstition."

The Catholic student meets a problem here which he should not ignore: the question of impartiality in writing Church history. A century ago Sir William Hamilton wrote that "Church history has not yet been written as alone written it ought to be—with truth, knowledge and impartiality." The Scottish philosopher is speaking particularly of Protestant Church historians, and his analysis of the then current Protestant history of the Reformation is a merciless arraignment of its method of concealing the truth. "Church history," Hamilton says, "falsely written, is a school of vainglory, hatred, and uncharitableness;

truly written, it is a discipline of humility, of charity, of mutual love." The historiography of Catholic history, too, has in its list many authors "who have sacrificed truth to partisan feeling, to private passion, or to earthly interests. But who are they? The Luitprands, Matthew Parises, Fleurys, Racines, and others whom good Catholics hold in detestation, but whom the Protestant world applauds, honors, almost claims as its own." The Lutheran historian Gruber reckoned Fleury one of the most important witnesses to the Protestant truth, because his Gallicanism was so unmanageable that he seemed rather to wish to destroy the papacy than to describe it. Impartiality presupposes the existence of a highly developed spirit of critical inquiry.

The Catholic logic of history recognises the spirit of criticism, welcomes it, does not fear it, accepts its findings when these are in strict conformity to truth; and, indeed, as in Leo XIII's celebrated letter of 1883, it points out to the spirit of critical inquiry methods for its own perfectioning. Father Kent—the "W. H. K." of the London *Tablet*—has examined the question in his *Catholic Truth and Historical Truth,* and Feder has dealt with it at length in his *Lehrbuch.* Too often, as the Catholic student will find by experience, the cry for impartiality on the part of non-Catholic historical writers amounts to this: they are to be free at all times to make their narrative of Catholic history a *chronique scandaleuse* of the Church's past; Catholic historians are accepted or rejected in proportion as their narrative gives in detail those unhappy and unfortunate episodes of the past which accentuate the human element in the Church; but no Catholic historian must conclude from this that he is at liberty to depict Protestant leaders or Protestantism itself in the same so-called impartial way. Denifle and Grisar discovered this attitude in our generation.   Gasquet has been trailed for a score of years by a writer whose historical logic consists in disproving a truth by an accumulation of scandalous pages on defections from that truth. Our own Lea is the best American example of this application of an ancient theory of Protestantism—*cujus regio, ejus historia*.   The student who is interested in the problem should read Professor Burr's reviews of Pastor's volumes on the *History of the Popes* in the *American Historical Review*.   Kent sums up the problem as follows:   "There is a strange fallacy involved in the suggestion that there can be any discrepancy or antagonism between Catholic truth and historical truth.   Doubtless there are many human systems that cannot afford to face the fierce light of history without some protecting screen or some reflecting medium.   And their advocates may well wish to doctor the crude facts and mitigate this force. But the champion of the Catholic Church should not stoop to such unworthy weakness. *Whatever record leaps to light she never shall be shamed.* It is her place to live in the light, while those who assail her shall perish in the darkness."

The statement that one is impartial in his quest of the truth or that one desires or intends to be impartial does not create a magical state of mind full-fashioned with that gift. The historical mind must be trained. The historical genius may be born—*poeta nascitur*—but a genius like Gibbon comes but once in a great epoch. The historical-mindedness of the Catholic student needs to be trained, if for no other reason, as Abbé Hogan states in his *Clerical Studies,* than that "his greatest peril is in dealing with historical characters with which he is out of sympathy." It is impossible to love the Church, to dwell in affection on the pages of her long history, and at the same time to admire the men who have apostatized from her communion and have in consequence rended the seamless robe of Christ, apparently for all time. But once accepted, the historian must reveal to us the man himself, the whole man with his good qualities as well as his defects. In his *Life of St. Philip Neri* Capecelatro states that this lack of impartiality is the chief weakness of many ecclesiastical biographers. In a little known treatise on the historical method—the preface to the *Acta Sanctorum*—the rule for historical truth is given in these carefully chosen words: "Profiteor me quae de Sanctis tradita litteris repererim dare, nihil asserere, nihil mutare, nihil meopte ingenio emendare, nihil praecidere, integre omnia ac inviolata afferre, quoad possum."

To reach this intellectual perfection is the precise work of the historical method. To be simple in describing the method of the historical sciences is to risk being obscure or commonplace. It is a help, of course, to define the method in an elementary way by saying that "the work of the historian may be summed up under two heads: first, there is the process of analysis; and secondly, one of synthesis." But from this step to the next is a high one—too high for the ordinary beginner, who can progress in his acquirement of the method only by easy stages.

The elements of the historical method are all older than the systematized science itself. The earliest treatises on method were not occasional or accidental in their issuance. Bodin's *Methodus ad Facilem Historiarum Cognitionem* (1566) was published at a time when the modern world was in the first thrilling ecstasy of the changes occurring all about it. The rapid spread of the art of printing had created an almost incalculable increase in the supply of books and an equally great demand for the printed page. The discovery of new lands and the age of exploration which followed brought a new light to Europe on almost every question within man's ken. The world conquest had begun; wealth was increasing; knowledge began to reach out to far wider bournes; caste and class distinctions were being transformed with corresponding changes in the political situation. A commercial revolution which is known better today, and better estimated in its relationship with other movements such as the Renaissance and the Protestant Revolt, was finding its way to every part of the Old World. The avidity with which scholars devoted themselves to the study of nature and of the past of the human race sent scores into libraries and archives to learn the secrets of that past from the sources themselves.

Nature and history—around these two foci turned the inquisitiveness of the age. Bodin responded to the logical query how best that past might be known. Bodin was followed by Keckermann, in his *De Natura et Proprietatibus Historiæ Commentarius* (1610). The Bollandists not only gave a concise evaluation of the method, but by that method itself inaugurated modern critical historical science. Descartes' *Discours de la Méthode pour bien Conduire sa*

*Raison et Chercher la Vérité dans les Sciences* appeared in 1637. Lenglet du Fresnoy gave his generation an excellent manual—*Méthode pour Étudier l'Histoire* (1713). Le Moyne's *Art both of Writing and Judging of History* appeared in French in 1670 and in English in 1695. These treatises, together with many others that might be mentioned, are feeble productions, when compared to a work like Bernheim's *Lehrbuch.* But they show how eagerly the critical spirit was searching for a systematic method for the historical sciences. The rise of what has since been called the *Hilfswissenschaften,* or auxiliary sciences of history—particularly the sciences of diplomatic, paleography, chronology, philology and archeology—for the most part the work of the Benedictines of St. Maur, brought within the range of the method a more profound knowledge of the aims and value of historical criticism.

The nineteenth century was the great century of historical development. No phase of history or of its methods of investigation and of criticism escaped the interest of scholars. The science was ready for Bernheim's treatise in 1889, and it is significant that the divisions he made of systematic historical training have not been changed since.

Nowadays it is well-nigh impossible to satisfy the canons of historical composition without a strict adherence to historical method or method-ology. "We shall have better history teaching," says Professor Fling, "when we have trained teachers; and we shall have the trained teachers when the teachers themselves, and those who employ them, realize that history can be taught only by those who have been prepared for the work." Freeman has pointed out that in his time things had not been going well in the teaching of history, because too many higher educational institutions, and especially the colleges of England, imagined that any intelligent person could teach history without special training. No one can be a successful student of any science, unless he has gone through the laboratorial processes of scientific analysis and has learned the resultant methods of the science itself. Historical method is, therefore, the laboratory where the student learns how to study history and how it may best be imparted either in the class-room or by means of writing. Bernheim's classical work on methodology not only sums up all that had been hitherto written on the subject, but remains the point of departure for all subsequent studies on the historical method. His volume marks an epoch in the science of studying history.

Bernheim begins his volume with an exhaustive study on the meaning and definition of History, and on its relation to other sciences, such as Philology, Politics, Sociology, Philosophy, Anthropology, Ethnology, the Natural Sciences and Art. He then divides the work up into parts: 1. *Methodology,* or the fundamental principles and procedure of arriving at certitude in the study of history; 2. *Heuristic* or *Quellenkunde,* the knowledge of the bibliographical sciences, the sources, and the auxiliary sciences of history; 3. *Historical Criticism,* or the question of the genuineness of the sources, their provenance and value, and the critical arrangement of the facts thus established in their physical and social environment, or the philosophy of history; 4. *Interpretation;* 5. *Methods of presentation,* or the artistic form of the historical narrative.

Professor York Powell says in his preface to Berry's English translation of Langlois-Seignobos: "Whether we like it or not, history has got to be scientifically studied, and it is not a question of style but of accuracy, of fulness of observation, and correctness of reasoning, that is before the student." History has come to be less a department of literature, less an ammunition source for controversialists, and more the serious study and the sincere and faithful utilisation and interpretation of documents for acquiring a correct knowledge of the past. The first lesson the historical method teaches us is, that without authentic sources no real history can be written;

and the second lesson it teaches is, where to find and how to use historical material. Where known sources have been destroyed or where known sources, to which access is denied, cannot be used, the present method of historical science will not allow the student to manufacture facts or to draw inferences. At the outset, therefore, by means of that department in methodology known as the bibliographical sciences, the student will learn what sources are known on this subject, what their nature is, and where they may be found.

The next scientific operation which is required  in the study of the documentary materials, is helped and guided by what German scholars call *Hilfswissenschaften,* and the French, *Sciences auxiliares.* These auxiliary sciences, or satellites of history, as Professor Freeman calls them, "are studies whose results are most precious to the historian, but which, in themselves, apart from their use to the historian, seem not to rise above that kind of curious interest which may be called forth by any inquiry to which a man gives his mind." When the student, therefore, has succeeded in gathering his material either in the original or in copies—photographed, printed, or copied by hand—he will find himself at a loss how to proceed unless he call to his help one or more of the auxiliary sciences. "It may be," says

Fling, "a manuscript that he has before him, and it may be incumbent upon him to determine its genuineness before using it. The performance of such a task would call for a knowledge of paleography, or the science of writing, of diplomatic, or the science of documents, and perhaps several others. If it is known that the document is genuine, the student must at least have a knowledge of the language in which it is written in order to interpret it. For some periods, such a knowledge is not easy to acquire. The investigator in the field of Grecian, or Medieval History must have a knowledge of philology, or the science of language. He must be acquainted with all the changes that take place in the meaning of a word in order to understand how it is used at a particular time. When the student comes to criticise his sources, and to determine their value, he finds that a knowledge of psychology is necessary; in arranging his facts, he must make use of chronology; in combining them, of logic; in forming the background, he is aided by geography, ethnology, economics and sociology; and in searching for the deeper meanings of historical development, by philosophy. These are the most important of the auxiliary sciences. There are, of course, many others, determined by the peculiar nature of the subject investigated."

The first set of operations under the general

title research or heuristic includes, then, historical bibliography and the auxiliary sciences. The second consists of an analysis of the source-material found by the bibliographical system and prepared by the canons of the auxiliary sciences for the further work of analysis or historical criticism. Historical criticism has as its object the questions of authenticity and interpretation. The third series of operations consists of a synthesis of the source-materials. The facts taken from them are properly authenticated and adjudicated, and the interpretation of the casual relationship between the fact or institutional factors is given in a composite whole. This is called historical composition.

A graphic design would be as follows:

A. RESEARCH WORK.—Search for source-material (Heuristic).
    I. Introduction to the Historical Method.
    II. Historical Bibliography.
    III. The Auxiliary Sciences.
B. HISTORICAL CRITICISM.—Analysis of the Materials.
    I. External Criticism (Provenance).
        1. Testing the Genuineness of the Source.
        2. Localizing it in time and place.
        3. Analyzing, editing, or restoring it.

II. Internal Criticism (Interpretation).
1. Determining the Value of the Source.
2. Interpreting its contents.
3. Establishing the historicity of its facts.

C. HISTORICAL COMPOSITION.—Synthetic operations.
1. General and Special Historical works.
2. Monographs.
3. Historical Dissertations.
4. Publication of Sources, etc.

Langlois-Seignobos, for example, in their *Introduction to the Study of History*, have followed practically the same system. The volume is divided into three Books. The first Book on Preliminary Studies introduces the student to the methods of research for documentary material, and to the auxiliary sciences. The second Book, on the Analytical Operations, touches upon the following subjects:

Introduction: General Conditions of Historical Knowledge.

Section I: External Criticism.—
1. Textual Criticism.
2. Critical Investigation of Authorship.
3. Critical Classification of Sources.
4. Critical Scholarship and Scholars.

Section II: Internal Criticism.—
1. Interpretative Criticism (Hermeneutics).
2. Negative Internal Criticism of the Good Faith and Accuracy of Authors.
3. Determination of Particular Facts.

The third Book, entitled Synthetic Operations, contains five chapters on the following topics:

I. General Conditions of Historical Construction.
II. The grouping of Facts.
III. Constructive Reasoning.
IV. The Construction of General Formulæ.
V. Exposition.

The logical outlines of these two treatises should be familiar to the student for the reason that so many books on the subject of the historical method are based on them. LANGLOIS-SEIGNOBOS quite naturally have the post-graduate French student in view. Father VILLADA makes his volume a special appeal for historical research into the history of Spain. VINCENT, in his *Historical Research*, has the needs of the American student before his eyes. FONCK has the group-idea of the Seminar in mind in his little volume. FEDER asks a rather thorough knowledge of philosophy and of historiography from his reader. BENIGNI writes for the finished theologian. Abbé

BLANC'S *Introduction* requires much study and meditation, while COLLINS aims at being attractive without being superficial and succeeds much better than many books in English. BERNHEIM writes a text-book for teacher and pupil and writes so well that he has not been superseded. There is then no dearth of manuals for the student of the historical method, be he a beginner or a finished scholar.

To grasp fully the entire force of the method, the student has need to keep before him a syllogism which runs somewhat like this: 1. The law of history is to speak the truth, the whole truth, and nothing but the truth, without fear or favour. 2. There is no manner of inquiry, as Abbé Hogan writes, "in which the truth is so liable to be disregarded or missed, nor in which so many things conspire to mislead the inquirer," as in the historical inquiry. "Wrong standards, ignorance, passion, prejudice, likings, dislikes, all tend to pervert men's judgments, and blind them to the most obvious features, sometimes to the reality of the most unquestionable facts. Extending to persons and things of the past the same feelings of sympathy or antipathy as to what surrounds us, we are all exposed to view them in the same way, exaggerating, consciously or unconsciously, the qualities of those we like and the faults of those we dislike, or conversely, hiding from others and from ourselves the faults of the former and the virtues of the latter." Church history, written by loyal and devoted children of the Church, is more liable to those two malicious spirits—the *suppressio veri* and the *suggestio falsi*—than any other branch of history, because the sympathy of the student is pledged at the outset to the good name, the honour, and the defence of the Catholic past. 3. Hence, in no aspect of the historical sciences is greater caution needed in the search for the truth, and stricter adherence to the laws of the historical method, than in the study of Church history.

To ensure the student against every tendency that might beget unfairness or partiality is the object of the method. In their effort to accomplish this, the historical sciences have reached out far and wide into the realms of knowledge and have constituted as essential or integral parts of the edifice of history many branches of science from allied fields. This will be evident from the brief descriptions which now follow:

## I. HISTORICAL BIBLIOGRAPHY

A tentative definition of historical bibliography would embrace three elements: the different classes of source-material, the different instruments of research, and the practical organization of research-work. The science of historical bibliography has for its object to indicate the method to be followed, and the helps to be used, in research-work. The different classes of research-material may be roughly divided into Sources and Historical Works. Sources may be either narrative, documentary, literary, or archeological. Historical Works may be either general or special; that is, without any given limits, or restricted to the limits of time, place, or idea. The instruments of bibliographical research may be manuals, repertories, dictionaries, encyclopedias, or bibliographies, all of which are designed to enable the student to learn quickly and accurately what source-material exists upon any given subject, and to suggest to his imagination other possible depots for such material.

To take an example: let us suppose that a student has chosen for his subject, *The Rise of the Catholic Hierarchy in the United States* (1763–1808). His first duty is to understand clearly the limits of time, place and idea contained in that title. He must understand why the years 1763–1808 are selected. He must visualize graphically either in his mind or upon a map which he has drawn up specially for that purpose, the extent of the "United States" during those years. He must have a very definite idea of what is meant by the term: *Rise—of—the—Catholic—Hierarchy*. Following the simple division of bibliographical helps—repertories, didactic books, and periodicals, a search through the articles cognate to his subject in the *Catholic Encyclopedia,* for example, would give him a more or less clear idea of the subject and would introduce him to the historical works on the subject. These he would quickly learn, are either general or special. A general work would be SHEA, *History of the Catholic Church in the United States,* Vol. ii (*Life and Times of Archbishop Carroll*), New York, 1888; a special work would be RUSSELL, *Maryland, the Land of Sanctuary* (Baltimore, 1907), or GUILDAY, *Life and Times of John Carroll* (1922). These works would lead him into the realm of source-material, and by diligent search, he would soon be able to draw up a bibliographical list of all the printed and unprinted material for his subject. For printed material the student would find as indispensable the Roman Documents on the question published by Professor Fish in the *American Historical Review,* Vol. xv (1910), pp. 800 to 829—*Documents relative to the adjustment of the Roman Catholic Organization in the United States.* A further search would reveal the translation of these documents by Father Devitt, S. J., in the *Records* of the American Catholic Historical Society, Vol. xxi (1910), pp. 185–236. Step by step, the student would clear a pathway for himself through all the printed material on his subject, and would bring his researches up to date by ransacking all the historical periodicals in order to make sure that he had missed nothing for his subject. There would remain still the real field of his research work—the unprinted material. With the aid, for example, of the Carnegie *Guides* he would be quickly put in contact with the location of this material, and personal search in such collections as the Baltimore Archdiocesan Archives, the Westminster (London) Archdiocesan Archives, and other collections, such as those at Georgetown University, and the Catholic Archives of America (Notre Dame University), would round his researches. With photograph-copies from Rome, Paris, Simancas and Seville, of all documents bearing on this subject, the next problem would be the practical method of putting all this material into shape for the work of Historical Criticism, and later, of Historical Composition.

The bibliographical helps for history in general, or what are called the *instruments de travail,* are entirely too numerous to be mentioned in detail. It will suffice to say to the student who has a definite object in view in his research-work that with a little systematic effort he can sieve the whole mass of source and book material in such a way as to be practically certain that nothing has escaped his notice. The instruments of bibliographical research ready for his use are usually divided as follows:

I.  General Bibliographies (for all the sciences).

1.  Universal bibliographies.
2.  Historical bibliographies.

3. Chronological bibliographies.
4. National bibliographies.

II. Special Bibliographies (for the science of history).

1. Bibliographies of the historical method.
2. Bibliographies of the auxiliary sciences.
3. Bibliographies of the philosophy of history.
4. Bibliographies of universal history.
5. Bibliographies of particular history.
   A. Bibliography of general history.
   B. Bibliography of special history (Institutions).
   (a) Constitutional or political history.
   (b) Law.
   (c) Economic problems.
   (d) Literature.
   (e) Art.
   (f) Sociology.
   (g) Religion.

Under this last division of religious history, which, in general, is the history of the different creeds of humanity, we have in a restricted sense ecclesiastical history, or the history of the Christian Church. A noteworthy attempt to cover the whole field of ecclesiastical history from the bibliographical viewpoint is the work of CHARLES DE SMEDT, S. J., *Introductio Generalis ad Historiam Ecclesiasticam* (Ghent, 1876). The modern text-books especially those of Hergenröther and Funk, contain bibliographical references in abundance; but no complete bibliography of ecclesiastical history, containing a systematic guidance for the student, has ever been published. The reason is obvious. One has only to make use of CHEVALIER, *Repertoire des Sources Historiques du Moyen Age,* to realize that it is folly for any one scholar to attempt such a work. The necessity of selection in the mass of historical literature is best seen in Paetow's *Guide to the Study of Medieval History* (1917). Each student of ecclesiastical history is, practically speaking, obliged to make his own set of cards. Beginning with a universal bibliography, such as STEIN, *Manuel de Bibliographie Général,* the student quickly sees that the next, and one might say, the indispensable, volume for his desk is LANGLOIS, *Manuel de Bibliographie Historique.* With the aid of Langlois, he learns the best books to be consulted for general bibliography, and is further orientated into the field of national bibliography. Here he learns that what Pirenne, Monod, Dahlmann-Waitz, Wattenbach, Gross, and Altamira have done for other countries, the authors of the *Guide to the Study and*

*Reading of American History* have done for the United States.

The third class of bibliographies—that of guides and lists for special subjects—is indicated in chronological and national bibliographies, and attention will be drawn to the principal bibliographical lists for Church history in another chapter.

Historical bibliography as the first clearing-house in the student's work of research should be so thoroughly mastered that all secondary sources shall have been seen and evaluated and the way opened for the real work of history—the search for further material in the shape of printed or unprinted documents. "The historian works with documents. Documents are the traces which have been left by the thoughts and actions of men of former times. . . . There is no substitute for documents; no documents, no history." The majority of unprinted historical documents are now preserved in archives, libraries, and museums. The critical study of this documentary material has given rise to a group of sciences, some of which are indispensable to the historian, and are therefore called the auxiliary sciences of history. These are: philology, diplomatic, paleography, chronology, and geography. Other sciences subordinate to these are brought into the circle as subordinate helps.

## II. AUXILIARY SCIENCES

The progress which has been made in the science of history is due for the most part to the more profound study in recent times of original manuscript sources. These sources Reusens has divided in his *Eléments de Paléographie* (1899) into two general classes—official documents and annals. Under the head of official documents he lists pontifical documents, imperial acts, acts of bishops, princes, municipal authorities, notaries etc. Under annals he mentions chronicles or histories composed by contemporary or quasi-contemporary writers. To utilize these sources according to modern scientific method, the student must be able:

1. To decipher and to read all such documents (Paleography).
2. To judge their authenticity from their external and internal character (Diplomatic).
3. To assign to them an exact place and precise date (Geography and Chronology).

It has been the tendency of the special student in the historical field to separate these main auxiliaries into sciences apart from the general study of history itself, and the rather rapid development of these subordinate studies has created a tendency to augment their number. Books have multiplied in all the auxiliary branches, and it is quite possible that, with their arrival at a definite stage of development, the much discussed problem of the scientific nature of history may be settled.

Of all the problems which present themselves in the study of any document, the most important is that of its authenticity. To gather the documents upon any one episode in history, to transcribe them, and to accept them as evidence without subjecting them to a searching criticism, both as regards their authentic nature and their value, is a thing of the past.

"The kernel of all sound teaching in historical matters," writes Freeman in his *Methods of Historical Study,* "is the doctrine that no historical study is of any value which does not take in a knowledge of original authorities. . . . Any knowledge of history which is good for anything must be founded on the mastery of original authorities; but it will not be founded on an, attempt to master all original authorities. Every student must master some; no student can master all. Even he who makes historical study the main business of his life cannot expect to master more than the original authorities for a few specially chosen periods."

Since everything depends upon the sources, these must be examined for every portion of the subject, in order that the historian may ascertain the degree of trustworthiness they contain and the value of the information he has culled from them. Although not all the auxiliary sciences are necessary for the student of ecclesiastical history, nevertheless a knowledge of their laws and a more than superficial acquaintance with their literature will give to his work a firmer solidity and a more scholarly appearance.

History is in reality the meeting-ground of all the sciences, and no avenue towards a complete knowledge of the subject in question should be barred. For the ecclesiastical historian the chief auxiliary sciences are: Philosophy, and especially Scholasticism; Theology, both dogmatic and moral; Canon Law, which, properly judged in its relation to Church history, is the Gospel of Christ in actual practice amongst Christians; Liturgy; and Hagiography. Theology is of supreme importance. It is unscientific to separate Church history and theology. One of the seven capital offenses of Modernism was the false concept of a possible distinction between the Christ of dogma and the Christ of history. Theology creates in the mind and heart of the historian an instinct which guides and an atmosphere which clarifies, without which false quantities are visualized and unwholesome judgments are formed. If it be true, as Melchior Cano has said, that the theologian "should be well versed in history, as is shown by the fate of those who, through ignorance of history, have fallen into error," it is equally true that the historian must be permeated with a true theological concept of the relations between the natural and the supernatural, between nature and grace, between the ordinary and the miraculous, if his judgments are to be true to the divine plan of creation and if his examination of the human side of the Church's activities is to be given its proper and unexaggerated place in the life-story of the object around which all his investigations are centred. In all advanced ecclesiastical historical work, theology and philosophy must be assumed as already forming a part of the student's general culture. Apart from these major auxiliary sciences, there are a certain number of subordinate helps, which are equally indispensable.

## 1. *Paleography*

It is not in a spirit of skepticism, but with a sincere desire to know the truth, that nowadays everything begins and everything ends with the scources. These original sources may be narrative sources, documentary sources, or archeological sources. In any good manual of historical bibliography, such as that of Langlois, the student will find an excellent guide for his search among these different classes of original materials. In a general way, it may be said that narrative and literary sources (or books) are mostly to be found in LIBRARIES, although in some cases, such as the Vatican Library or the National Library in Paris, manuscripts as well as books are to be found therein. Archeological sources are usually kept in MUSEUMS, but care must be taken not to define the term too rigidly; the British Museum, for example, is principally a library of books and manuscripts. Documentary or manuscript sources are usually housed in ARCHIVES. The Vatican Archives, the Archives des Affaires Étrangères (Paris), the Archivo General de Indias (Seville), the Archivo General de Simancas (Simancas) the Public Record Office (London), the Royal Bavarian Archives (Munich), the Bodleian Archives (Oxford), the Manuscript Section of the Library of Congress (Washington), and many others, are examples of these manuscript centres.

While the science of paleography cannot be confined solely to manuscript sources, nevertheless for all practical purposes its scope may be limited to the work of deciphering old documents taken from these general archival centres. Manuscript sources are one of the treasure-houses of all accurate knowledge of historical events and movements. In his *Paläographie und Hand-*

*schriftenkunde,* Lehmann has observed that paleography is a combination of knowledge, ideas,
methods, and discipline, which enable one to read
old writings correctly and without danger of error,
to determine their age, their provenance, and their
value, and to understand and explain whether erroneous factors have crept into such writings.
Paleography differs from diplomatic—the science
of the genuineness of a document—in this: that
the former teaches us how to transcribe and interpret correctly written documents, while the
latter helps us to distinguish what is genuine
from what is false in a document.    Among the
subsidiary or allied sciences of paleography are:
epigraphy, the science of inscriptions, graffiti,
etc.; sigillography (sphragistics), or the science
of seals; numismatics, or the science of the
*legenda* on money and medals; iconography;
papyrology; the science of miniatures; crypto-
graphy; tachygraphy; the science of hieroglyphics
and cuneiform writings; and the science of musi-
cal paleography or plain chant.   The division of
paleography into these subsidiary sciences dates
from the nineteenth century, and the term itself
nowadays is applied almost entirely to documents
written on papyrus, parchment, and paper.

Dom John Mabillon, the leader of the Benedictine historical   school   of   St.  Maur  (1632–

1707), has the honour of having raised paleography to the dignity of a distinct science, in his famous work *De Re Diplomatica,* published at Paris in 1681. The first great step in the development of paleographical studies was taken by the *École des Chartes,* in Paris, founded in 1821, for the training of archivists. Since that time, the science has occupied a permanent place in higher education. In Germany, von Stein founded a society for the publication of the *Monumenta Germaniae Historica,* and the paleographical school which was begun to carry out this undertaking, soon brought the science into all the German universities. In Austria, Sickel imitated the methods of the *École des Chartes* in the *Institut für österreichische Geschichtsforschung* established in Vienna in 1854. In Italy, the reorganization of paleographical studies began with the opening of the Vatican Archives. A glance at any bibliographical list will show how profoundly Italian scholars have entered into this study. In Belgium, the pioneer in the work was Canon Reusens, who inaugurated the study at the University of Louvain, in 1882. From Germany, France, and Belgium, the science was received into England and America.

Steffens' *Lateinische Paläographie* divides the study into five periods:

**A.** The Handwritings of Roman Times.

1. Capital (square and rustic) writing i–vii cent.

2. The earlier Roman Cursive (i–iv cent.).

3. Uncial writing (vi–xi cent.).

4. Later Roman Cursive (iv–ix cent.).

5. Semi-uncial writing (v–viii cent.).

**B.** The National Handwritings.

1. Old-Italian (v–xiii cent.):
    (a) Old Italian Cursive writing;
    (b) The writing of the Papal Chancery;
    (c) Old Italian Book Hand;
    (d) Lombard-Benevento Book Hand.

2. Merovingian Handwriting and Book Hand (vi–viii cent.);

3. Visigothic Handwriting (vii–xii cent.);

4. Irish and Anglo-Saxon Script (v–xvi cent.).

**C.** The Carolingian Minuscule Script (ix–xii).

**D.** The Gothic Minuscule (xii–xvi cent.).

**E.** Humanistic and Modern Gothic Script (xvi–xx cent.).

The historian sees in these changes from one handwriting to another, guide-posts, as it were, along the centuries. The old majestic capitals of the Roman empire with their accompanying cursive for rapid writing, which is in reality a sort of simplified capital hand, gave way to the national writings after the barbarian invasions. The cursive underwent a further change in this, that smaller letters (*minusculae*) were used, and from this minuscule arose the different writings called Lombardian, Merovingian, Visigothic, and Anglo-Saxon. These names have more than a geographical signification. The Carolingian style of handwriting stands as a memorial to the beauty of Charlemagne's various reforms, which nowadays go under the general term of the Carolingian Renaissance. The spread of the Irish missionaries in England and on the Continent, where they erected monasteries and centres of learning from Quentovic to Rome, chief of which were the schools at Toul, Fontaine, Luxeuil, St. Gall, Plaisance, and Bobbio, brought into the civilized world, then in the throes of the invasion, one of the most powerful influences for culture which ever existed. The Irish monks were the leaders in the Carolingian Revival. The copy of the Gospels known as the Book of Kells, for example, stands apart in the realm of paleography as the finest example of the period. The Caroline minuscule soon predominated throughout Europe, but about the twelfth century, a new form came into use, known as the

Gothic. This was the form used in the first printed books. It was less round and less graceful in outline than the Caroline. The influence of Humanism in the fifteenth century caused an equally strong change in the handwriting of modern Europe, and it effected a gradual return to the old Roman minuscule. With the invention of printing, books took the place of manuscripts, and each country gradually developed its own modification of type, whether Caroline or Gothic. In Germany, the old Gothic Script is still largely used; and the modern writings in use are hardly more than a development of the forms introduced at the Renaissance. Bibliographical lists for the sciences of paleography will be found in Steffens' and Reusens, and in Prou's *Manuel de Paléographie Latine et Française.*

## 2. *Diplomatic*

The science of Diplomatic has for its object the study of the historical value of documents. The word *diploma* is sometimes taken in a generic way to include the different kinds of documents which come under the historian's gaze: charta, charte, notitia, epistola, littera, scriptura, acta, instrumentum, testamentum, chirographum, scriptum, documentum, roll, chartularium, register, contract, etc. etc. Most of these classes of documents have characteristics which differentiate them one from another; but certain aspects of them are common to all, and among these aspects one is of the highest importance to the historian, namely, their authenticity.  Diplomatic is the science of the authenticity of such documentary evidence.  Documents are valuable only for direct historical evidence when they can be proven to be authentic, coming to us from a known source and a definite time and place.  To verify the authentic character of a document, to determine its provenance and to establish its time and place of composition, are all necessary preliminaries to the use of the document as historical evidence.

The question of authenticity is the most delicate of the three, and it is owing to the efforts of historical students to reach certain fixed rules for such verification that we invoke the auxiliary science of diplomatic.  The authorship and the date of the document are not always so important that they need to be known with exactitude, but until the document is proven genuine, there can be no question of its use for direct and immediate evidence.  Any written document may justly be called a diplomatic source of history, and the science which has grown up around the problem of the authenticity of such sources furnishes the student with the definition, the principles and the methods to be used in studying the provenance of such sources, in interpreting their meaning, and in determining their value as historical material.

It is quite possible, as Bresslau has said in another connection, that one can become a skilled worker in the field of history without being a diplomatist; but if the scientific ability which the science of diplomatic creates and nourishes in the student be absent, there will surely be discrepancies in his method of interpretation and valuation. Vincent has expressed this thought clearly in the following paragraph: "Although one may never devote himself to a period in which Latin documents are the rule, with the intention of becoming an expert diplomatist, it is nevertheless essential that one should be familar with the evidence and method by which conclusions are reached. Even for the reader who depends upon the printed copies it is necessary to know the construction of documents and the practices of chanceries, so that he may distinguish between what is formal and what is freshly communicated. For even if it is left to the paleographers to determine whether a document is genuine or not, there are certain parts of the paper which are historically more valuable than others, and the student should be able to decide what are merely notarial repetitions and what are expressions of will, or relations of fact. And in the case of the writing, each period has its own peculiarities of expression, varying slightly from its predecessors. These have been so carefully studied that documents may be identified and dates established in large measure by the evidence of form. The office practice of every reign in the medieval empire has been classified by modern scholars, and by the combined application of paleography and diplomatic the world has been put into possession of a mass of sifted materials which were inaccessible to the earlier historians."

Through these principles, the student is able to discover, establish, and verify the authenticity of the documents he wishes to use. Giry has given a classic mould to these principles in his *Manuel de Diplomatique*. His volume is divided into seven books which deal with the following subjects: 1. the object and history of the science; 2. technical chronology; 3. terminology of the document (persons, places, measures, language); 4. the organic structure of the document; 5. chancelleries; 6. unofficial documents; 7. forgeries. It is in defining the organic structure, or in explaining the constituent elements of a legal documentary source that the science has reached its highest development.

Apart from these general indications, the science of diplomatic embraces also the following questions: sources of documents; language of documents; different stages in the construction of legal documents; methods of transmitting and preserving documents, and laws for the detection of forgeries. Of the additional questions with which the science deals, an important one is that of the chancellery system of the courts of Europe; and for the Church historian the Papal Chancellery is more important still.

To give an adequate bibliographical apparatus for this science is impossible in a brief survey. The means and methods of research in archival centres grow in value year by year, and any general manual, such as that of Giry, contains lists of guides, general catalogues, regesta, and collections for this purpose. The richest of all these bibliographies is that of Oesterley, *Wegweiser durch die Literatur der Urkundensammlungen*. Giry gives a list of the facsimiles, which had been published up to his time, in the chronological order of the publication. The multiple problems of the science of diplomatic constitute an ever-increasing literature on the subject. These can be followed in the bibliographical section of the *Revue d'Histoire Ecclésiastique*, of Louvain.

### 3. *Chronology and Geography*

Chronology and geography have been called the two eyes of history, without the use of which all is confusion and uncertainty. There are two general branches in the science of chronology—mathematical (theoretical, astronomical), and historical (technical). Mathematical chronology is that part of the science of mathematics which determines the rules, to be used in measuring time. Technical or historical chronology, of which we treat here, has for its object the system of authenticating the dates given in the documents and of bringing these dates, if necessary, to their corresponding place in our system of computing time. Up to modern times, as we can see at a glance, from the pages of Giry's *Manuel de Diplomatique,* chronology was a confused mass of systems and methods. There have been not only different methods of computing the eras, but also many diverse systems of numbering the cycles of the year, the days of the month, and the parts of the day. Now, the date, as has been observed, is the most indispensable single factor in the study of a document, both from the historical as well as from the legal point of view.

A knowledge of the systems of time-calculation employed in the Middle Ages and in modern times is, therefore, a *conditio sine qua non* of historical research. The year was begun, for example, in different parts of Europe, on January 1 (Style of the Circumcision); March 1 (Style of Venice); March 21 or 22 (Style of the Vernal Equinox); March 25 (Style of Annunciation); August 11 (Style of Denmark); September 21 or 22 (Style of the Autumnal Equinox); December 25 (Style of the Nativity); Easter (Style of France). There were also, under the Julian Calendar, the divisions of the months into kalends, nones, and ides; and the much-used divisions of indictions—a relic of the days of the Roman Empire, when the year was divided up into units of fifteen for the purpose of revising the collection of taxes.

These various modes of beginning the year, not only in different countries, but even in the same country, have caused the confusion which would still be resting on the science of technical chronology, had it not been for the great classic of the Benedictines of France, *L'Art de Vérifier les Dates,* which was begun under the direction of Dom Maur d'Antine, and continued by Dom Clemencet and Dom Durand, who published the first edition of the work, in Paris, in 1750. Dom Francis Clement revised the work and published subsequent editions in 1770, and in 1783–87. A fourth edition was published by

Saint-Allais between 1818–44, in two separate forms: one in forty-four volumes octavo, and the other in eleven volumes folio. One of the first scholars to attempt a reform of this science was Joseph Scaliger, in his *De Emendatione Temporum* (1583), which has since become the basis for all chronological study. In 1627, Petaŭ, better known for his theological works, published his studies: *De Doctrina Temporum* (1617), and *Rationarium Temporum* (1633). One of the most complete of all the manuals on chronology is that of C. Ludwig Ideler: *Handbuch der Mathematischen und Technischen Chronologie* (1825–26), of which a short compendium exists: *Lehrbuch der Chronologie* (1831).

We see the sun rise in the morning, Ideler says in the preface of his *Handbuch,* we see it reach its full zenith at midday, and withdraw itself from our sight in the evening, and during the time of its "coming and going" we have been living through parts of the day, month, year, and era, as humanity has done since the beginning of creation. The attempt to measure these periods of time has given rise to several sciences, and among them chronology has attempted to place order in the series of centuries which have gone by; for no surer test of the authenticity of a statement or the genuineness of a document exists than the perfect agreement of any two or more dates which may be mentioned therein.

There are few subjects of an erudite nature, says another writer, of greater utility to the historian and at the same time fraught with thornier difficulties than that of technical chronology. The first difficulty to be borne in mind by the student of Church history is that a very important change was effected in our system of time-calculation by the Bull *Inter gravissimas pastorales officii nostri curas,* of Gregory XIII, February 29, 1582. The errors in the Julian method of computing the year and the discrepancy which existed between the astronomical year (as sustained by mathematical chronology) and the ordinary reckoning in use amounted, in 1582, to ten days, so that the Julian system, introduced by Cæsar (45 B. C.) had fallen ten days in arrear. The alteration made by Gregory XIII, since known as the New Style (often abbreviated to N. S.), and as the Gregorian Calendar, consisted in this: that by pontifical law the fifth of October, 1582, was to be called the fifteenth. St. Teresa's feast day, although she passed away in reality on October 5, 1582, is now celebrated October 15. Gregory XIII also determined that the year should begin all over the western world on the same day, January 1. In order to prevent the Julian error from causing an arrear in the future, he ruled that three leap years should be omitted in every four centuries, namely, those of the centennial years the first two figures of which are not exact multiples of four, as 1700, 1800, 1900, 2100, etc.

For the purpose of ascertaining the exact dates of documents, it is important to remember when the New Style was adopted in the various countries of Europe. Denmark, France, Spain, Portugal, Italy (not wholly), Holland and the greater part of Belgium, and Lorraine adopted the Gregorian Calendar in 1582; in Germany and Switzerland the Catholic provinces adopted it in 1584; the Protestant provinces in 1700; in Poland it was adopted in 1586; in Hungary, in 1587; in Tuscany, in 1749; and in Great Britain and Ireland, in 1752. Since the Catholic life of the United States has been more closely united with that of Great Britain and Ireland, especially in the days before the organization of the hierarchy (1607–1789), some confusion has occurred from the discrepancy of the time-computation made at London and at Rome—our chief ecclesiastical centres during this period.

Of all the subsidiary helps of history none owes so much to ecclesiastics and to their love of science as geography. One might almost claim that the science of geography developed side-by-side with the missionary activities in the Church from the beginning. Otto Hartig's article on *Geography* in the *Catholic Encyclopedia* will furnish the student with an excellent résumé of the great histories of geography by Humboldt, Peschel, Ritter, and Saint-Martin. Zurla's volume, *Dei Vantaggi della Cattolica Religione derivata della Geografia*, published at Venice, in 1825, is the earliest account of the subject from the Church historian's viewpoint.

Practically all the greatest geographers the world has seen were priests and religious; and in all the different branches of the geographical sciences—cartography, astronomy, physiography, meteorology, volcanology, thalassography, etc.— the best known names are those of Catholic priests and religious: Adam of Bremen, John de Plano Carpini, William Rubruck, John of Monte Corvino, Bede, Virgilius, Albertus Magnus, Roger Bacon, Cardinal Peter d'Ailly, whose *Imago Mundi* was a favorite book of Columbus, Fra Mauro, Canon Waldseemüller, whose map of 1507 gave the name America to the western world, and Copernicus, a canon of the church of Frauenburg, the renowned Polish astronomer, who is the acknowledged discoverer of the heliocentric system, and many others, the fore-runners of the famous Jesuit astronomers, mathematical geographers, and ethnographers, and of the geographer and ethnologist, Father Wm.

Schmidt, S.V.D., whose discoveries, as developed in the famous periodical, *Anthropos* (Vienna), have won for him and his school the unanimous applause of the scientific world. Beazley's splendid study of the question—*The Dawn of Modern Geography*—will introduce the student to this field of knowledge, and prepare him to deal with a difficult problem which must enter into his interpretation of the past: the influence of geography upon the history of a people, or the physical causes which have exerted a moulding force in the institutional life of the race.

### III. HISTORICAL CRITICISM

Criticism has not always borne a good name. Historical criticism became prominent at a time when the so-called higher criticism of the Scriptures was enjoying its day of notoriety; and the rather dubious reputation the latter acquired in circles where the Bible was revered as the Inspired Word, cast a shadow upon the value of the former as a constructive science or inquiry into the truth.

We see an evidence of this in the Introduction of Père Delehaye's book on the *Legends of the Saints*. "Historical criticism," he says, "when applied to the Lives of the Saints, has had certain results which are in no way surprising to

those who are accustomed to handle documents
and to interpret inscriptions, but which have had
a somewhat disturbing effect on the mind of the
general public. . . . If you suggest that the biographer of a saint has been unequal to his task,
or that he has not professed to write as a historian, you are accused of attacking the saint
himself, who, it appears, is too powerful to allow
himself to be compromised by an indiscreet
panegyrist. If, again, you venture to express
doubt concerning certain marvellous incidents re-
peated by the author on insufficient evidence,
although well calculated to enhance the glory of
the saint, you are at once suspected of lack of
faith. You are told you are introducing the
spirit of rationalism into history, as though in
questions of fact it were not above all things essential to weigh the evidence. How often has
not an accusation of destructive criticism been
flung, and men treated as iconoclasts, whose sole
object has been to appraise at their true value the
documents which justify our attitude of venera-
tion, and who are only too happy when able to
declare that one of God's friends has been fortunate enough to find a historian worthy of his
task."

What the well-known Bollandist says, somewhat caustically, it is true, of hagiography, holds
equally well for ecclesiastical biography in gen-

eral. To detect inferior workmanship in what we already possess, to clear the road of the mass of rubbish which has not only hindered the progress of knowledge, but which has been allowed to stand as certified history, to insist upon a technical method of research, of criticism, and of composition in all that is offered to us, is absolutely necessary if Church history is to be protected against historiasters of the future.

Church history is or ought to be a subject too sacred to the deepest feelings of faith and of patriotism for anyone to enter into the field without a well-balanced judgment on the value of the sources at his disposal. All data furnished to him by former writers, by tradition, or by archival depots must be tested, in order that the truth or error they contain may be known and appreciated at its proper value. To test is to criticise; and while criticism is not the chief end of historical research, still, no conclusions may be made by the research-worker until all his material has been put through the sieve of historical criticism.

In his *Historical Research*, Professor Vincent says: "The processes of criticism fall naturally into two parts. The first important step is to determine whether the given source is at all admissible as evidence, or, in other words, whether the material is genuine or not. Conclusions are

worthless and labor is wasted if the document
is fraudulent or misjudged.  It is necessary to
know at the outset whether the chronicle, charter,
or relic is in reality what it claims to be, or what
it has been esteemed to be.  It is important to
determine where and when it originated, who was
its author, and whence he derived his information.
The rules of procedure by which these facts are
determined in historical research constitute
*External Criticism.* . . . The second part of the
critical process weighs the relation of the testimony to the truth.  One must decide whether the
statements made are trustworthy and, if not
absolutely certain, whether they are probable.
The degree of probability or possibility must be
determined or, if necessary, the whole cast out
as worthless.  This is *Internal Criticism,* and is
often called Higher Criticism, since it deals with
more important matter than external criticism."

1. EXTERNAL CRITICISM is that part of the
historical method which determines the authenticity of the source.  The document is somewhat
like a prisoner at the bar.  Its genuineness must
be tested, where possible, by paleographical
and diplomatic criticism.  It must be localized in
time and place.  It must be ascertained, whether
in its present state it exists exactly as its author
left it.  In order to test its genuineness, the student must ask himself if it is what it appears to

be or if it is a forgery. One is too apt to imagine that historical forgeries passed out of style with the Middle Ages. The document must be viewed from every possible angle. Its agreement or disagreement with facts known from other genuine sources of the same place and period, or on the same subject, will often be a factor decisive of its authenticity. The writer's ignorance of facts which he should have known and which should have been mentioned in the document, or the record of events which he clearly could not have known at the time of writing, are other signs of genuinity or of its absence. A document proven probably genuine by these tests can often be heightened in value by an analysis which may restore it to its original state, or which may accentuate the historicity of the facts it contains.

The False Decretals, or the Pseudo-Isidorian Decretals, are a good example of the value of external criticism. Of the one hundred documents contained in the collection, which was compiled about 852, about five are authentic. It is by analyzing the Decretals and by localizing them in place and time, that the student is enabled to see the constant use of material which the Popes to whom they are attributed could never have known. Letters from the Popes of the first three centuries, for instance, contain parts of documents dating from the sixth, seventh, and eighth centuries. The importance of a strict test for historical material is easily recognizable when one reflects that these False Decretals, although a huge forgery, passed for genuine all through the Middle Ages; and when especially one touches the delicate question of how far these forgeries contributed to papal authority in that period. The sum total of all these operations will give the student a fair idea of how far his source or sources may be trusted as authentic. A further question arises—whether the material facts found in the source can be used as evidence for the work in hand.

2. INTERNAL CRITICISM is that part of the historical method which determines the historicity of the facts contained in the document. It is not of absolute necessity that the document be proven genuine; even forgeries or documents with truncated truths may contain valuable material. But before any conclusion is admissible, the facts contained in the document must be tested. In order to determine the value of these facts, the character of the sources, the knowledge of the author, and the influences prevalent at the time of writing must be carefully investigated.

We must first be certain that we know exactly what the author said and that we understand what he wrote as he understood it. It would be misleading, for example, to see in the words *lex, homo,* or *scutagium* of the Magna Charta (1215) the same meaning as they bear in classical Latin dictionaries. Moreover, the facts given by the author or writer must be firmly established as having taken place exactly as reported. The student or research-worker must be permeated with an earnest desire to reach the truth and must be, as far as it lies within his power, indifferent to the results of his inquiry or criticism. What is of the utmost importance in dealing with any source, whether it be a volume already in print or a document hitherto used or unused by historians, is that the student jealously guard himself against the danger of making it agree with preconceived conclusions of his own.

In their *Introduction,* Langlois and Seignobos warn the student that criticism is antagonistic to the normal bent of mind: "The spontaneous tendency of man is to yield assent to affirmations, and to reproduce them, without even clearly distinguishing them from the results of his own observations. In everyday life do we not accept indiscriminately, without any kind of verification, hearsay reports, anonymous and unguaranteed statements, 'documents' of indifferent or inferior authority? It requires a special reason to induce us to take the trouble to examine into the origin and value of a document on the history

of yesterday; otherwise, if there is no outrageous
improbability in it, and as long as it is not contradicted, we swallow it whole, we pin our faith
to it, we hawk it about, and, if need be, embellish
it in the process.   Every candid man must admit
that it requires a violent effort to shake off
*ignavia critica,* that common form of intellectual
sloth, that this effort must be continually re-
peated, and is often accompanied by real pain.
The natural instinct of a man in the water is to
do precisely that which will infallibly cause him
to be drowned; learning to swim means acquiring the habit of suppressing spontaneous movements and performing others instead.   Similarly,
criticism is not a natural habit; it must be in-
culcated and only becomes organic by dint of
continued practise."

Consequently, historical work is preëminently
critical, and whoever enters upon it without having first been put on his guard against his instinct
is sure to be drowned in it.   It may not be necessary for the student to set for himself rules of
such geometrical rigidity as Descartes has done;
for methodical distrust towards all statements
contained in the documents he uses, or an
*a priori* suspicion that they are erroneous, may
not always be the safest path to follow to the
discovery of truth.   In ecclesiastical history, at
any rate, a certain power of sympathetic under-

standing is essential to any real insight into the period in question.

Enough has been said to emphasize the value and the necessity of historical criticism. The different processes already alluded to may be summed up as follows:

I. External Criticism.
   1. Testing the genuineness of the source.
   2. Localizing it (time, place, author).
   3. Analyzing it (recension and restoration of text).

II. Internal Criticism.
   1. Determining the value of the source.
   2. Interpretation of the source.
   3. Establishment of the facts.

In his *Institutions du Moyen Age,* a privately printed manual which Canon Cauchie gave to his students at the University of Louvain, the subject of historical criticism is dealt with in a somewhat different way, though essentially the processes are the same. He defines criticism as the art of discerning the true from the false, and divides the work into three parts: 1. *Connaître la provenance des sources.* 2. *Les comprendre.* 3. *Déterminer la valeur de leur renseignements.* In other words:

1. External criticism or provenance of the sources (lower criticism, erudition, material criticism).
   (a) Direct or immediate provenance, or the criticism of authenticity
   (b) Indirect or mediate provenance, or the criticism of originality
   (c) Reconstruction of the primitive text or the criticism of integrity
2. Internal criticism or historical value of sources.
   (a) Analytical interpretation (hermeneutic or exegesis, philology.
   (b) Evaluation of the source, or criticism of authority.

Besides the works already mentioned, there are many books on the subject of historical criticism; space prevents any attempt at completeness in these pages. BERNHEIM's fourth chapter (pp. 325–332) contains a good bibliography and LANGLOIS-SEIGNOBOS give other works not included in BERNHEIM. The classical work on the subject before BERNHEIM was CHARLES DE SMEDT, S. J., *Principes de la Critique Historique.* On the history of the growth of critical historical studies, the student will do well to consult the second part of LANGLOIS, *Manuel de Bibliographie Historique,* and for special reference to America, JAMESON, *History of Historical Writing in America.* Other works of reference on the subject are H. A. GEORGE, *Historical Evidence;* MACE, *Method in History for Teachers and Students;* DROYSEN-ANDREWS, *Outline of the Principles of History;* ACTON, *A Lecture on the Study of History delivered at Cambridge* (1895); and FREEMAN, *Methods of Historical Study,* Lecture III, *The Nature of Historical Evidence.*

Once awakened and properly guided at the start, the spirit of critical inquiry not only grows with each fresh exercise, but also acquires in the true historian a marvellous delicacy of touch. "He sees," it is Abbé Hogan who speaks, "often intuitively what is spurious and what is genuine. He determines with accuracy the amount of credence to give to all manner of statements that come under his notice. His judgments often differ from those of the uninitiated, nor can he always fully justify them, but he feels them to be right. . . . To sum up: historical criticism implies judgment, perspicacity, insight, a gift for sifting evidence, for weighing testimonies; a certain literary sense enabling the student to discern what documents are genuine and what spurious, what is primitive in them, and what a later addition; a quickness to see what is likely or unlikely in a given time or place, what narratives are trustworthy or the opposite, what is real and what is fanciful in the connections established between facts and the conclusions drawn from them."

## IV. HISTORICAL COMPOSITION

The work of historical composition may be understood to embrace the whole of those synthetical operations, some of which make up the remote preparation for the final draft, and others of which are of proximate value for the same. The remote preparation starts where the process of analysis leaves off. All analysis properly organized begins under definite and almost rigid limitations. "The operations of history are so numerous, from the first discovery of the document to the final formula of the conclusion, they require such minute precautions, so great a variety of natural gifts and acquired habits, that there is no man who can perform by himself all the work on any one point." These limitations are generally of time, place, and idea. Placing boundaries to the subject beforehand gives a reasonable restraint upon the research-work, especially on the bibliographical field, and at times a limit to the process of critical interpretation.

For beginners in the scientific study of history, limitation is one of the surest safeguards. Historical research familiarizes the student with the general and special knowledge necessary for his subject. Historical criticism supplies him for his work with a mass of isolated facts, which have more or less stood the test of investigation. But the net result of these operations cannot be called history. The facts gathered must go through a process of synthesis, before the real work of historical exposition can be started.

It is this process of synthetic operations which we call the remote preparation. The general conditions of historical composition are based upon the principle that "the mode of construction cannot be regulated by the ideal plan of the science we desire to construct; it depends on the material we have at our disposal. It would be chimerical to formulate a scheme which the material would not allow us to carry out; it would be like proposing to construct an Eiffel Tower with building stones." The process of analysis, when completed, may, indeed, "leave a student of history with a body of disjointed and disconnected facts," but it is too much to say, as Seignobos has done, that the synthetic operations must necessarily begin with "an incoherent mass of minute facts, with detailed knowledge reduced as it were to a powder." The mind cannot help grouping the facts obtained. The limitations which the student places upon his research, gradually bring into relief in his own mind the natural

grouping of time, place, and idea; and the over-
lapping which occurs with any one of these divisions, already sets the loom of history in
motion.  It is true that the page will lack the
one element which makes history readable, that
is, reality, unless the facts found are visioned by
the student in their original setting.  Imagination plays an important part in combining different elements of fact knowledge, and when all
the facts at one's command are thus revivified,
grouping must be done, very largely again under
the influence of imagination.  The gaps which
occur between facts or between groupings of
facts call for something more serious than vision.
Logic has to be applied, and historical reasoning
brought into action.  Little by little, classified
groupings emerge with more and more distinct-
ness, and from these groupings a species of general reasoning can be drawn which leads up to
formulas or conclusions.  Hence, the four stages
in the process of historical construction:—(1)
the visioning of the facts; (2) the grouping of
the facts; (3) constructive reasoning; (4) the
construction of general formulæ.

All this however, does not complete the process.  This is what is called the *mise en œuvre*
of the materials.  So far, the constructive process
merely arranges the *matériaux* for the last stage
of historical work; namely, exposition.  "A little

thought," says Collins, "will show how frequently this last step is left unfinished; how many there are who seem to be able to produce materials for history, but not to write history. Nor is it only a question of the possession and the utilization of a good literary style. Many who have this cannot write history, and many who have it not can yet do so; for from this point of view, as we have said already, style is nothing but the vehicle for the presentation of the work to the world after that work is in effect complete. What is really needed is that the facts should be digested and systematized until they have their right perspective and their right proportion: a perspective and proportion which will depend indeed upon the point of view, but which, when this is once taken up, have a real existence. Then they must be presented in such a way as to form one whole with a unity of its own, just as the elements of a landscape combine to form one whole, or as the elements of a picture ought to combine to form one whole."

Exposition can be said to demand mainly three things: a plan, sincerity, and the power of expression.

The materials at one's command and the purpose in view will naturally dominate the plan of the work. There must be a well-balanced proportion between the materials and the viewpoint.

The viewpoint in historical writing has undergone changes, and historians have not all the same conception of the end aimed at by historical work. Hence the "mode of writing history" is not and has not been a constant one. The three main schools of historiography are the narrative, the didactic, and the genetic. The narrative school of historians has as its aim "to preserve the memory and propagate the knowledge of glorious deeds, or of events which were of importance to a man, a family, or a people." So much religious history is still written from this standpoint that its value has little that is permanent. This is the easiest kind of history to compose, for the chronological "mode" usually provides a cloak for large gaps in historical facts and in historical reasoning. Most Church histories are written in the simple narrative style with an occasional use of the didactic.

When facts are selected because they are useful in business, in politics, in religion, or in education, or when the search is for precedents to enlighten statesmen or churchmen, for arguments to support a cause or a theory, or for ethical ideals to surprise the world, then we have the so-called didactic conception of history. In its narrative and didactic forms, history was considered more as a branch of literature than as a distinct science with its own laws and cus-

toms.  Then the change which came about the
middle of the nineteenth century, when the strict
methods of procedure in other sciences were
applied to history, gave rise to the science of
historical research, and to historical criticism.
It brought also into being a new type of historical composition—the historical monograph
with all its scientific apparatus of notes, references, and *pièces justificatives*.  The third
school which cannot be said to dominate history
writing outside the Universities, is the genetic
or development school.  Its cornerstone is criticism, and it is this all-ruling fact which keeps it
from becoming popular.  "Uncritical histories of
the narrative and didactic types are still being
produced.  There are still those who demand that
history shall first of all be literature.  There
are others, the majority of schoolmasters among
them, who demand that history shall first of all
convey lessons in morality or patriotism, or social
service.  There are others, and here must be included a large part of the legion described as 'the
general reading public,' who demand of history
only that it shall be interesting.  To many of
these the very idea of scientific history with its
destructive criticism, its denial of the right of
personal bias, and its sober gray of fact, amounting in many cases to a mere balancing of prob-

abilities without definite conclusions, is somewhat repugnant."

Scientific history too often called itself evolutionary or history acting under the principles of evolution, and has appeared too often as if guided by some of the false standards of "Higher Criticism," for it to be given the place of honour among those who see in Church history nothing more than the accurate narration of human events. The ecclesiastical historian cannot hold fast to the aim which should be present in his work if the genetic mode alone be followed. Events are to be related, it is true, with the strictest accuracy possible, and general formulæ or conclusions are only to be drawn in strict conformity with the rules of logic; but beyond this comes the moral lesson for the present and the future.

The mere recital of the discovery of America, the story of its colonization, its birth as a nation, its wars, and its progress, is not American history. There must be running through the pages of the book we put in the hands of our children the living fire of love for their country, of admiration for the great men of the past, of honest appreciation of the shabby side of our history, and above all the spirit of patriotic purpose in the upbuilding of their character as citizens of the land. No less and no more is asked of Church history. Honesty, sincerity, and impartiality must never be absent from the narrative. The lessons drawn from the past must never be exaggerated—*qui nimis probat nihil probat*. But in every case the facts offered must be substantiated from sources which have stood the test of criticism.

The term, power of expression, so far as historical writing is concerned, is not synonymous with rhetoric. It is far better to present a subject with truth, clearness, and precision, unadorned by the art of rhetoric than to compose a well-written essay filled with inaccuracies and faulty conclusions. Rhetoric is not to be despised, but if the style is exact, clear, moderate, in good taste, and elegant, and if the reader realizes that the principal thing which has guided his author is love for the truth, the work in question is not far from perfection. James F. Rhodes, in his paper *Concerning the Writing of History,* lays stress on originality: "An historian, to make a mark, must show some originality, somewhere in his work." The best originality in the field of historical writing, now, as ever in the past, is the originality which seeks the truth, the whole truth, and nothing but that which clarifies the truth. In the long dynasty of historians from Herodotus to our own day, very few deserve the *tulit punctum* for sheer honesty.

The process of the historical method from the beginning of the search for materials on through its various phases of criticism and of a synthetic establishment of the facts and their exposition is a kind of torch that lights and guides the student through the obscure pathways of the past to truth itself. *Per aspera ad astra*—there is no royal road to historical truth, no magic formula that will open up the silent watches of the past. In the night that is over lie many hidden things which no man will ever discover, and many others that can be known to us only as through a glass in a dark manner, while others await the painstaking labour of a devoted scholar who brings to the search a trained mind, a generous heart, and a love for those who have lived their lives and have gone before us, their work accomplished and their fame, perhaps, waiting upon the searcher of those forgotten records where their deeds are covered with the dust of time.

In the formation of the Catholic historian many obstacles may arise to slacken the student's original ardour and determination. The cause is a lofty one—to make known to his generation some portion of the Church's past. History never stays written. Every epoch "demands a history written from its own standpoint—with reference to its own social conditions, its thought, its beliefs and its acquisitions—and therefore comprehensible to the men who live in it." More particularly today does the world need religious history in order to find its way back to religious belief. Not that Church history is to be made, even by strict adherence to the scientific method of its analytical and synthetic processes, merely a means for the religious appeal; but, certainly, a means to convey to the minds and hearts of our generation the knowledge that only within the Catholic Church, as every page of its great past shows, will the heart of man find the link that logically unites the supernatural and the natural, only within the bounds of submission to her doctrine will complete intellectual liberty be found, only in the eternal lessons taught to the world by her philosophy can the balance be kept between the material civilization about us and the spiritual destiny for which we have been fashioned by the Creator.

It is the purpose of the careful and cautious processes which have gone towards the formation of the historian to act as a restraint upon the legitimate enthusiasm the Church historian cannot help feeling for his subject. The mass of historical literature through which he must go step-by-step will of its very nature arouse in his mind sentiments and even principles of caution which tell him that he can never master it in its entirety. He must at some moment in his researches and in his critical analyses of documentary source-material bring this first part of his work to an end, simply because it may be endless. This will act as a check upon his interpretation of the facts before him—facts usually established as historically genuine only after a prolonged scrutiny of the witnesses or the testimony upon which they are based. Then, again, in the *enchaînement* of his facts there is a subtle danger—the ease with which comparisons and identities, contrasts and oppositions fall into place in his narrative. This arouses a pressing hesitancy which is valuable to the historian in reaching conclusions.

And beyond all this—there is the historian himself. He is, with all his science, the result of influences innumerable. "So many things happen to bias our opinions and vitiate our taste that the strongest resolutions to impartiality will prove insignificant, unless we carefully guard against those temptations whereby men are not only daily surprised but, as it were, driven into errors and mistakes: ignorance, education, religion, passion, and party-disputes are in a kind of conspiracy to seduce mankind." Even when the historian feels that he has reached a state of impartiality which gives him freedom to discuss in a faultless way the casual elements in the subject he is describing, he must remember Bishop Creighton's warning: "The writer who strives to avoid any tendency becomes dull, and the cult of impartiality paralyzes the judgment."

No one in our own times so clearly estimated the need of Church historical studies as Pope Leo XIII. In his letter on historical studies of August, 1883, to Cardinals de Luca, Pitra, and Hergenröther, the Holy Father has written a striking summary of the duty involved in the choice of Church history as a field for intellectual activity: "Often indeed, children have manuals put into their hands for instruction thickly sown with falsehood, and when they become accustomed to these, especially if the perversity and heedlessness of the teacher countenance it, the young students are easily turned against venerable antiquity and imbued with an irreverent scorn of things and men most holy. On leaving the elementary classes, they are frequently exposed to a danger even greater; for in the higher studies, from the narrative of facts they rise to the examination of causes; and from these causes they endeavour to deduce laws issuing in rash theories, often in flat contradiction to divine revelation, and with no other motive than that of glossing over or concealing the salutary influence which Christian institutions have had on the course of human destinies and the progress of events. . . . It is indeed hard to conceive how

much harm may be done by the subservience of
history to party ends and to the ambition of in-
dividuals.   For it becomes, not the guide of life,
nor the light of truth, as the ancients have rightly
declared it ought to be, but the accomplice of
vice and the agent of corruption, especially for
the young, whose minds it will fill with unsound
opinions, and whose hearts it will turn away from
virtue and modesty. . . . Let bare assertions be
replaced by the fruits of painful and patient research, judgments rashly made by the outcome
of serious study, and frivolous opinions by the
criticism of wisdom.  Strenuous efforts should
be made to refute all falsehoods and untrue
statements by ascending to the fountain-heads of
information. . . . Arbitrary opinion must give
way before solid arguments; truth in spite of persistent opposition must triumph in the end; it may
be darkened for the moment; never can it be
extinguished."

# CHAPTER VI

### THE MISSION OF THE CATHOLIC HISTORIAN [1]

The fantastic scene between the Archdeacon Claude and Louis XI, of France, as portrayed in Victor Hugo's *Notre Dame de Paris,* may be cited to students and readers of history as a fair example of that prophetic vision which the historian should enjoy in order to look backward through the centuries for a just and equitable estimate of progress in this field of intellectual development. The King, disguised, had come with a boon companion to Dom Claude's cell for consultation. The conversation soon turned to books, and Louis asked: "Where are your books?" Opening the window of his room and gazing out upon the imposing edifice of Notre Dame, Claude replied: "There is one!" Then placing his hand upon a newly-printed book bearing the date 1474, he added: "And here is another. Alas, the printed book will be the death of the book in stone—*ceci tuera cela: le Livre tuera l'Eglise!*"

If it be permissible to garner a lesson from the

[1] Presidential Address, December 16, 1924. before the American Catholic Historical Society, Philadelphia.

244

pages of an enemy-book like *Notre Dame de Paris,* then the whole rhapsodic chapter which follows this scene is worthy of our serious attention. With wondrous skill the novelist develops under the title *Ceci tuera Cela* the idea that with the advent of printing should come the close of the Church's reign over the lives of her children by means of those great books in stone—those perfect encyclopedias of human learning—her cathedrals of the middle years of the Christian epoch.—The Press should bring an end to the Church—Hugo almost sings it as a threnody—*la Presse tuera l'Eglise!*

It was to be Gutenberg against the imperial power of ecclesiastical Rome, with victory all along the centuries for the bold invader. It was to be man with this new toy wonderfully arrayed against God—this time with conquest certain. It was to be at last the building of a triumphant Tower of Babel for the human race to reach a new paradise of its own planning: without God. The presses of the world were to multiply in numbers and in force like the waves of an ever-rising sea. There would be a second deluge, a deluge of knowledge, of new learning, in which all the past should be swept away and mankind would be able to begin anew its tremendous history without the restraints of belief, of authority, or of such outworn historical factors as the alleged visible presence of God on earth in the person of the Vicar of Christ.

An epoch now approaching its term of five hundred years in length lies between Gutenberg and our day. Viewing it as a period of struggle and of polemic contest for mastery between the two books—the one of stone, the other of paper— we can recognize as its primal lesson the fact that since the great cleavage of the sixteenth century the printed book has been used by the opponents of the Catholic faith with no more direct and no more potent success than in the domain of history. Newman has argued this fact so conclusively in his *Lectures on the Present Position of Catholics in England* that impartial scholars hesitate no longer over his uncompromising conclusion: by wholesale, retail, systematic, unscrupulous lying,—for he could use, he says, no gentler term,—many rivulets were made to flow for the feeding of the great Protestant tradition, that tradition which has been and is still little short of one vast pretence or fiction, the substance, the force, the edge of which is slander.

Slander on a truly magnificent scale to prove the greater purity of Protestantism: such must be the impartial judgment passed upon that series of volumes with which the battle of the two books began.

In his *History of Modern Historiography*,

Edward Fueter is justified in asserting as a premiss that modern ecclesiastical historical study is a daughter of the Lutheran Rebellion against the papacy. In one sense all historical study previous to the sixteenth century falls within the field of ecclesiastical history; in another and truer sense, the Church and her scholars can be said to have done very little up to the Lutheran Revolt to relate her history; and that when the historical attack was made from Magdeburg as a centre, the Church was not prepared for the contest. In this latter view most modern historiographers concur. It was the collapse of religious and political unity in the western world and the subsequent conflict with the symposium of errors formulated by the Protestant divines that awakened in the Catholic ranks a consciousness of the value and necessity of ecclesiastical history as a weapon of defence for the faith. Even this judgment, however, needs to be made softly. One cannot be certain whether the religious and political cleavage in itself and of itself would have awakened the dormant Catholic historian.

There was abroad at the time an attitude of indifference towards the Protestant rebels on the part of Catholic scholars, and this attitude has not changed much with the passing of the years. Protestantism as a world-movement has never been viewed seriously by that sixth sense of supreme values never absent from the Catholic theological outlook. It was incipiently recognized then, as it is more clearly understood to-day, after four centuries, that Protestantism, as an intellectual movement, is doomed to disintegration and is devoid of any inner constructive force which might leave a lasting impress on world progress. Protestantism brought no new doctrinal crisis into the Christian fold, but gained its inherent strength as a synthesis, gradually built up, of all the heresies of the fifteen centuries before its time. Arianism, Nestorianism, and Pelagianism still dominate in our theological treatises over the doctrinal values of Anglicanism, Calvinism, or Lutheranism.

It is problematical, therefore, whether Catholic Church historical investigation would have leaped so suddenly through Baronius into the forefront of intellectual activity had the Lutherans not centred their strategy of attack upon the historical past of the Church.

The great commercial revolution which reached its earliest peak in Luther's boyhood, the age of discovery and exploration which was fairly under way during his youth, the vast missionary enterprises with their valuable contributions to the study of ethnology, anthropology, and comparative religions, and the political growth of Europe's far-flung empire to the west and south of the globe—these, in themselves, would not necessarily have aroused a profound interest in the Church history of the past. This interest Protestant apologetics not only created and almost made its own, but also fashioned upon a scale that must ever win the admiration of the scholar. From the middle of the sixteenth century to our day, history has been in consequence the chief weapon of attack upon the Catholic faith. As a religious world-movement, the full-blown effect of Protestantism died with the closing scenes of the Council of Trent and the calling out of the spiritual forces which made up the Counter-Reformation. Even Trent, greatest of all assemblies in the Christian Church, neither appointed its own historian and thus left the field open to the apostate Sarpi, nor did it give an impetus to historical study, although the earliest critical attack from the Protestant side—Flacius' *Catalogue of Witnesses against the Papacy,* which appeared in Basle in 1556, must have been recognized by the Fathers of the Council as a change from the doctrinal to the historical in the Lutheran method of controversy.

The four centuries that separate us from this earliest use of history against the papacy have been crowded with a fierce and bitter *certamen utriusque ecclesiae,* in which the greatest scholars of both churches have been engaged. The

Lutheran historical attack found Catholic historians badly prepared. Some few works of a general character in Church history had been written before that time, but practically all studies in ecclesiastical history up to the sixteenth century were of a partial or particularist character.

Prior to the dominant Flacian movement in Lutheran polemics, the narration of the history of the Christian Church was meagre, both in value, and in outline. Some names, indeed, do stand out, prominent in all time for their brilliancy; and foremost among these is Eusebius, who died about 340 A. D. A survey of Church historians, such as is found in Nirschl or in Stang, reveals the fact that almost every historical narrative up to the Lutheran Revolt is of this fragmentary character.

Stang lists but one name in the second century—HEGESIPPUS, whose precious historical data are partially preserved in Eusebius. There is but one name in the third century—JULIUS AFRICANUS, some fragments of whose *Chronography* are likewise in Eusebius' *Ecclesiastical History*. EUSEBIUS himself is the outstanding Church historian of the fourth century; indeed of all the centuries since his day, with his immemorial title of "Father of Ecclesiastical History." His work does not pretend to be complete, however. It is not critical in our modern sense; but though

written under influences that might have set
bounds to its veraciousness, it is the most brilliant
production of the early Church. "It would be
difficult to overestimate the obligation which pos-
terity is under to Eusebius for this monumental
work. Living during the period of transition,
when the old order was changing and all connected with it was passing into oblivion, he came
forward at the critical moment with his immense
stores of learning and preserved priceless treasures of Christian antiquity."

Imitated by many Church historians after his
time, Eusebius found few worthy followers, until
the days of OROSIUS, who accepted, about 415
A. D., the burden given to him by St. Augustine
of Hippo, and compiled his *Seven Books against
the Heathen,* the first general history of the
Church we possess. The Church histories of
SOCRATES, SOZOMEN, THEODORET, and EVAGRIUS
are all valuable as continuations of the Eusebian
narrative. Orosius was likewise added to from
time to time and his work was used as the text-
book *par excellence* in the schools of the medieval
period. Its fame grew through the translation
into Anglo-Saxon which Alfred the Great made
of it in the ninth century for his people. To
this earliest period of Church historiography
belongs ST. AUGUSTINE's noblest work, the *City
of God,* written between 413 and 428. Augus-

tine's purpose was not to write a general history of the Church, but to answer the newest version of the old calumny that the spread of the Christian faith was responsible for the gradual disruption of the Roman Empire.

With the *City of God,* ecclesiastical history became largely apologetic in its character and philosophic in its interpretation of the past. Henry Osborn Taylor says of the work in his *Medieval Mind:*

In no province of inquiry does Augustine's apologetic purpose appear with clearer power than in his treatment of history, profane and sacred. Through the centuries the currents of divine purpose are seen to draw into their dual course the otherwise pointless eddying of human affairs. Beneath the Providence of God, a revolving succession of kingdoms fill out the destinies of the earthly Commonwealth of war and rapine, until the red torrents are pressed together into the terrestrial greatness of imperial Rome. No power of heathen gods effected this result, nor all the falsities of pagan philosophy; but the will of the one true Christian God. The fortunes of the heavenly City are traced through the prefigurative stories of antediluvian and patriarchial times, and then on through the prophetic history of the Chosen People, until the end of prophecy appears—Christ and the Catholic Church.

The *Civitas Dei* reigned as queen in the Catholic philosophy of history until the latter part of the seventeenth century when BOSSUET penned his incomparable study—*A Discourse on Universal History*. Bossuet's theme is the same as that described by St. Augustine: the idea of Providence ruling the affairs of men. No historian since his day has approached Bossuet in the sublime picture of his world-view of the past.

Between Augustine and Bossuet there lie a thousand years of medieval life, and what remains to be considered in ecclesiastical historiography is a vast collection of chronicles and annals, necrologies and *menologia,* histories of nations and abbeys, and lives of great men. In the general history of the Church, however, it is a period almost as arid as the plain described by the Prophet Ezechiel—a valley strewn with bones, very many and exceeding dry, with no genius to hearken to the voice that desired these bones to live. There are exceptions, of course— for we have in that long age the works of CASSIODORUS, of GREGORY OF TOURS, of BEDE THE VENERABLE, of PAUL THE DEACON, of ADAM OF BREMEN, to whom we owe our knowledge of the medieval Church in Greenland, and many others. But paradox as it may seem to be, in that age of the universality of Catholic thought and action, no serious attempt was made to compose a general history of the Church until about 1459, when St. Antoninus of Florence wrote his *Historical Summary*. This work is one of the most worthy historical productions of the Middle Ages.

Florence in the time of St. Antoninus, its Archbishop, was noted for humanistic studies. During the fifteenth century, especially under the Medici (1429–1492), the lovely Tuscan city was the intellectual centre of a new world of literary and historical criticism created by the humanistic movement. In Petrarch and Boccaccio the writing of history underwent an abrupt change. The age of purely narrative history was closing and that of history with a more critical attitude towards the sources was at its dawn. It is difficult to characterize this new history. Its tendency or its effect was the secularization of historical investigation, the emancipation of history from its ecclesiastical setting. Humanism has all the appearance of a pronouncedly anti-clerical movement in the field of letters. The humanists did not directly attack the bases of Christian faith, for that would have violated their attitude of studied detachment from the supernatural. But it was also the age of Macchiavelli (1469–1512) when the spirit of the time was rather to ignore the place of the Church in the world. While the most celebrated of all the scholars of the humanistic and early Renaissance periods is the learned but worldly Cardinal BEMBO (1470–1547), the name which links the medieval and the modern in the field of critical ecclesiastical history is that of LORENZO VALLA (1407–1457). There is nothing pleasing in the life or in the character of the celebrated critic whose treatise on the Donation of Constantine (1440) was of undoubted influence upon Luther's anti-papal writings.

Valla's *Declamatio* on the Donation was first published by Ulrich von Hutten in 1517, with a fiery preface against the claims of the Holy See. When Luther and von Hutten combined their anti-Roman purposes in the spring of 1520, the Revolt, to which the name Protestant had not yet been given, may be said to have assumed a clearer tendency. This tendency Luther emphasized in his *Address to the German Nobility,* issued in August of that year. This "ringing appeal" to the German princes and nobles to take in hand the social, moral, economic, and religious reformation of Germany, by placing the ax to the root of all their *gravamina,* namely, the temporal over-lordship of the Pope of Rome, was in reality the beginning of the great clevage itself.

The works of LUTHER are not remarkable for their historical insight. He displays in few of his pages a knowledge of the historical past of

Christianity, and there is scarcely a trace of the critical method of approach followed by the humanistic historians. If it is not, therefore, to Luther's works that modern ecclesiastical historiography can be traced, certainly to his spirit and perhaps to his immediate direction must be accredited the earliest books of Protestant Church history. The polemical nature of early Lutheranism necessitated an historical support for its break with the Catholic past, and this was the origin of the method followed since Luther's day. The rise of the new historical objective is understood the better, the more accurately we estimate Luther's place in the religious revolt. Grisar says that "at no other time, save possibly at the French Revolution, was mankind more profoundly stirred by the force of untried ideas which with suggestive power suddenly pervaded every rank of society. Scholars, writers, artists, countless men who had heard nothing of Luther that was not to his advantage, and who, from lack of theological knowledge, were unable fully to appreciate the spirit of his writings, were carried away by the man who so courageously attacked the crying abuses which they themselves had long bewailed." At the same time, it is a problem still unsettled by the historians how long the cleavage would have existed in the Christian world, had not the policy of vivid, human, unscrupulous historical attack upon the papacy, in language understood even by the lowliest, been adopted in Luther's own lifetime.

Protestantism could have chosen no more effective means of reaching the citadel of Catholicism. Fifteen centuries of Catholic conquest; for the defence of which there was no bulwark erected by the historians. It is a problem worthy of study just how far the Cleavage would have been possible, had the Church possessed scholars prepared to defend her historical past. Her Protestant opponents had stated in terms that might be caught by all, by the scholar in his study, as well as groups of peasants in public houses who watched the finger of the reader running along the page, the major premiss of the growing rebellion: namely, that the New Religion preserved in all its purity the ancient doctrines of the Church. It was logical that the method to be followed was so to sully and blacken the Ages of Faith during the medieval period, that all would recognize the Pope to be the Antichrist spoken of in the Scriptures, the Antichrist of Babylon, the Scarlet Woman, or the Mystery of Iniquity who had ruled for a thousand years by means of a wickedness surpassing all description. From that time to our own, the dull persistent suspicion against the papacy has remained, haunting the minds of otherwise impartial scholars—*res judicata pro veritate accipitur.*

That there has been a change—a change amounting almost to a revolution in our knowledge of the religious conditions of the sixteenth century, is well-known. Unfortunately, it is well-known only to the scholar. The results of the new critical school of historians lie to a large extent buried in technical reviews, in the doctrinal dissertations of the universities, or in languages the populace does not understand. This new viewpoint is known to historians, since they are the ones for whom historians write; but the great public, especially in America, which has been so profoundly influenced during four centuries by the Protestant tradition, remains oblivious to the change. The text-books of our colleges and schools, with rare exceptions, have not caught up with the work of the new school of historians; and so the solid mass of prejudice and ignorance which was set up as a *politique de la barrière* stands as it stood those days three and a half centuries ago.

Count Joseph De Maistre, who wrote a century ago, gave us an exact estimate of this animus against the papacy, and strove to change the attitude of the non-Catholic Christian world with his great work *On the Pope.* The three centuries of historical study before his day appeared to him as hardly more than one long conspiracy against the truth—*Depuis trois siècles, l'histoire entière semble n'être qu'une grande conjuration contre la vérité!* One has but to compare his scholarly work with the popular knowledge to-day to respond to the query how far the impartial historian has succeeded in changing the Protestant tradition. *Without the Pope there can be no Christianity*, De Maistre says, *and by an inevitable result, the attitude of the non-Catholic world towards the papacy wounds to the heart the social order of the world.* Learned circles are not entirely free from this century-old prejudice; for under a refined anti-papalism—voiced today in the modern political fetish of a disunion between Church and State—the hackneyed reproach of older ages lives on to harass loyal Catholics and to hinder scholarship from reckoning with whole-hearted impartiality "the tremendous force whose nature and workings should logically be their first and chief preoccupation in approaching the history of Europe during the past fifteen centuries."

That this attitude of mind is traceable to Luther is now accepted by all historians. It is even probable that Luther planned the anti-papal method of attack. As early as 1536, we find the initial Protestant diatribe, the *Lives of the Roman Pontiffs*, written by the apostate English Augustinian, ROBERT BARNES, one of Luther's intimates at Wittenberg, published with a preface by Luther himself. "I have been constrained by sorrow of heart," Luther writes, "and also by legitimate rage, to pour out all this in order that I might inspire other pious and Christian souls to investigate, as much as they can be investigated, the popish tyranny and the Pope's Church. For without doubt all those who have the Spirit of Christ know well that they can bring no higher or more acceptable praise-offering to God than all they say or write against this bloodthirsty, unclean, blaspheming whore of the devil. I for my part, unversed and ill-informed as I was at first with regard to history, attacked the papacy *a priori,* as they say—that is, out of the Holy Scriptures. And now it is a wonderful delight to me to find that others are doing the same thing *a posteriori*—that is, from history—and it gives me the greatest joy and satisfaction to see, as I do most clearly, that history and Scripture entirely coincide in this respect." Barnes had cast upon the Popes all the calamities, social, political and economic, that had happened in the past and glorified all as leaders of human liberty who had opposed the papacy.

The second work written under the anti-papal influence of Wittenberg was that of another apostate Englishman, the former Edwardian

Bishop of Ossory, JOHN BALE, an ex-Carmelite. His *Historical Summary of the Writers of Great Britain,* published in 1548, deals with 1400 authors, and the new pragmatic turn he gave the historical narrative was to emphasize, wherever possible, all expressions of hostility against the Popes found in their works. Bale who is generally known in the chronicles of the day as the "foul-mouthed," has been taken, along with Barnes, as the precursor of the classic historical polemic of early Protestantism—the CENTURIES OF MAGDEBURG. In the year before his death, Luther expressed a wish to see this anti-papal history organized upon a larger scale. "It would be a blessed thing to do," he writes, "if there were any who could do it, to strike out the Pope altogether as the arch-enemy of our Lord and Saviour, and the destroyer of His Holy Christian Church. Next to the Holy Scriptures, the histories of the emperors are well adapted to this end, for in them it is seen how full of devils the Popes have been and still are, and also what gross, ignorant asses they have always shown themselves as regards the Scriptures, to the eternal shame of the accursed see of Rome."

The first to respond to this exhortation was the theological heir of Martin Luther—MATTHIAS FLACIUS, the founder of Protestant Church history. Flacius was born in 1520, became a

Lutheran at the age of 19, and at 24 was made professor of Hebrew at Wittenberg. Owing to his opposition to the Interim of 1548, he quarreled with Melanchthon, and withdrew to Magdeburg, where he began the outlines for the *Centuries*. Flacius was Luther's heir also in the fanatical anti-papal spirit of Wittenberg. The remainder of his life—he died in 1575—was spent as the leader of the old Lutherans or Flacians as opposed to the Philippists, as the followers of Melanchthon were called. Flacius began his work by the publication, at Basle in 1565, of a *Catalogue of Witnesses for the Truth against Papal Claims*. The burden of the book which went through many editions in a short time, is that the Pope must be Antichrist. Flacius considered it his life's vocation to fight against the papacy and if possible to extinguish it completely. His spirit is that of Voltaire, two centuries later—*Ecrâsez l'infâme!* The *Catalogue of Witnesses* was a welcome source-book to the Protestant pulpiteers of the day, and its villainous anecdotes were soon common talk, even among the children.

Janssen in his *History of the German People* has given his readers several of the contemporary reactions to the book. One will suffice. In a sermon printed in 1590 by one of the Lutheran preachers, we find: "Although I had already before read, heard, and even seen much of the

villainies of the Popes, and so had been strength-
ened in my conviction that the Pope of Rome was
the Antichrist, yet, when I read this book I found
that papist iniquity was ten times worse than I had
ever imagined. . . . The Popes are neither men
nor gods, but real incarnate devils who far outdo
Satan in wickedness and rascality. If we were to
collect together all the infamous deeds of the
Popes recounted in histories, God help us, what a
monstrous book it would make. We should not
have enough ox-, cow-, donkey-, and calf-skins to
bind it."

*All the infamous deeds of the Popes*—such
might well serve as a sub-title for the *Centuries*
which Flacius called into being.

*The Book was at last to be the death of the
Church.*

To carry out his plan, Flacius created at
Magdeburg, an historical society composed of
five Editors or Governors, under whom laboured
two Architects and seven junior Research-
Assistants. The purpose underlying the *Centuries* was to prove by the use of carefully selected
materials that, from the death of the last Apostle
down to the restoration of the pure Gospel under
Martin Luther, the Christian Church had been
led astray by the Roman Antichrist. No work
since the beginning of Protestantism was so successful in downright villainy. We can pass over

the method said to have been used by Flacius himself, when traveling about, frequently in disguise, seeking admittance into the libraries of monasteries and churches, and cutting out parts of manuscripts with his knife, tearing out whole pages, or stealing whole books. The term *culter Flacianus,* the Flacian knife, and the *manus Flaciana,* the hand of Flacius, were proverbial for several centuries after his death. A "literary freebooter" Janssen calls him; and the remains of his pilferings and mutilations can still be seen in his library, now at Wolfenbüttel.

That there was, however, great merit in his design is admitted by a Catholic scholar who writes: "The plan of the *Centuries* was a noble one and as the work of the first among modern writers on ecclesiastical history who professes to treat the subject critically, it marks an epoch in Church history; its method, with its return to original sources, is quite sound, and the skill with which the vast masses of material were marshalled is worthy of all praise. . . . Yet noble as was the plan, the same cannot be said of its execution; virulent anti-papal abuse is common to the whole work. The exercise of the critical faculty is limited by the demands of anti-Roman controversy, and no attempt is made to take a calm and impartial survey of the Church's history. Its constant polemical tone, its grouping of facts

coloured by party spirit, its unjust treatment of
the Church, its uncritical accumulation of anti-
papal story and legend, made the *Centuries* for a
long time the arsenal of Protestant controversialists. . . . Through the ages no crime is too
monstrous, no story too incredible, provided it
furnish a means of blackening the memory of the
occupants of Peter's Chair."

No part of the Protestant world of the sixteenth century drank in more greedily the vulgar
and hearty word-pictures of the *Centuries* than
Great Britain. The earliest writer to be influenced by Magdeburg was JOHN FOXE, the
author of the notorious *Book of Martyrs* (1563),
which was based to a larger extent than is generally known upon the *Centuries*. Where the
*Centuries* slew its thousands, the *Book of
Martyrs* has slain its tens of thousands. The
influence of Foxe's book upon English Protestantism both at home and in the American colonies can never be fully estimated. Though inferior to the work of the Centuriators in critical
analysis, the martyrology of Foxe reached the
minds of English people in a way that has seldom
been equalled. Foxe was an inexhaustible source
for violent Puritan pulpiteering against the
Church, and his work forms one of the land-
marks in the stern background of many of the
colonial No-Popery laws. Foxe remains still the

foremost English Protestant apologist, the foremost among the Protestant masters in the art of
historical lying.  After Foxe, and considerably
under his influence, came JOHN KNOX, the Scottish reformer.  His *History of the Reformation
in Scotland* (1564) surpasses all the anti-papal
documents of the day in frenzied fanaticism.
Knox is the model of the fighting No-Popery
parson.  His anti-papal complex is more honest
than that of Foxe.  History to Knox is a constant combat between good and evil, between
light and darkness; and darkness was profound
upon the face of the Catholic deep.  With
Knox, the struggle against the Church of Rome
assumes its melodramatic place in English literature.  The sifting of the false from the true has
placed the work of Foxe among the slippery
sources of Protestant historiography; while the
influence of John Knox has been present at every
crisis in Great Britain and in America where the
two Christian bodies found themselves aroused
by a recurrence of the old-time hatred.

These are but a few of the early Protestant
historical apologists who belong to the Magdeburg dynasty.  Straight and true, like an arrow,
back through the years since the thirteen volumes
of the *Centuries* were published (1556–1564),
can be traced the Protestant apologetic which
these early writers and their congeners have

handed on to generation after generation as the principal stock in trade of the less-cultured non-conformist pulpits.

Truth, says de Maistre, in its combat with error, never becomes angry. In the enormous mass of historical works written by Catholic controversialists of the highest rank, such as Bellarmine, Suarez, Bossuet, and others, the reader will search in vain for the slightest tendency to personal diatribe or scurrility. The opposite is true with error, for error never preserves its impartiality in combating the truth. The *Centuries* contained within their own method the seeds of the disease from which they were to die a natural death. Protestant writers have laboured in vain, as, for example, von Wegele in his *History of History Writing in Germany* (1885), to save the *Centuries* from oblivion. But the famous Protestant arsenal lies in ruins today, though its baleful influence lives on outside the City of the Learned. A second edition was published by the Calvinists at Basle in 1624, but it has never been fully reprinted. Baur in his *Epochs of Ecclesiastical Historiography* (1852) is the last writer to have the courage to assert the critical value of Magdeburg scholarship.

The *Centuries* had, however, shown the way to Catholic scholarship, and before the second edition of the work was printed, there had been published at Rome between 1588 and 1607 what is in all likelihood the greatest of all Catholic historical works, the twelve volumes of the *Annales Ecclesiastici* of the Venerable Cesare Cardinal BARONIUS. The *Annals* are the first critical general history of the Church in modern times, and they have merited for Baronius a share in the title enjoyed by Eusebius—"Father of Ecclesiastical History." Behind the genius of Baronius stands the ever-charming figure of St. Philip Neri. It is to the founder of the Oratorians that the Church owes this precious legacy of documentary evidence for her fair name. Seven years in all, at Philip's command, Baronius preached weekly in the Churches of San Girolamo and San Giovanni of the Florentines in Rome sermons covering the whole range of Church history. Then there followed, again under Philip's direction, at times apparently harsh and unsympathetic, twenty-three years of research for source material, of critical analysis of texts, and of comparison of documents, before the actual composition of the work began. Though the composition was done single-handed, Baronius had awakened so much interest in his studies and the *Centuries* had created so much distress in Catholic circles, that no historical writer from his day down to the great historical collections of the last century enjoyed such world-wide assistance.

In the spring of 1588, the first volume was given to the public and it quickly won for its author universal acclaim. The second volume appeared in 1590, and after that volumes appeared as promptly as Baronius was able to write them amid his many and varied duties, until the last or twelfth volume which was completed just before his death in 1607. Baronius brought the history of the Church down to the accession of Innocent III, in 1198. Three fellow-Oratorians continued the *Annals* after the death of Baronius: Raynaldus carried the story to the year 1565, Laderchi to 1571, and Augustine Theiner to 1583.

With the publication of the *Annals* the Magdeburg *Centuries* were eclipsed. They are nowadays, as one writer has phrased it, "of interest only as a sunken landmark in the field of historical literature, and as the stimulus of Baronius' genius." The *Annals* have been the inspiration of all students of Church history since his day. The work of Baronius was not faultless. On many of the vexed historical problems, he was unable to say the final word, since all the documents on these questions were not available until centuries later. But he remains for all time the model of the ideal Catholic historian—characterized by unwearied research for authentic sources, unvarying loyalty to truth, accuracy of critical judgment, and objectivity in the presentation of historical events.

It would make the treatment of our subject very convenient to describe the growth of ecclesiastical history writing from the middle of the sixteenth century to the middle of the nineteenth under two distinct forms, or directed, as it were, by two distinct cycles—the Magdeburg and the Baronian. But the lines do not run parallel. In the Protestant churches, particularly in the Lutheran, a development took place which leaves these three centuries difficult to define owing to the maze of changes and counter-changes which came into the historical field from the camp of the philosophers. These changes have the appearance of abruptness, but they are in reality the logical development of the great cleavage itself. For a hundred years after Magdeburg, the Protestant churches were engrossed with domestic troubles; and in the disintegration which was bound to follow the abolition of religious authority, the three established churches —Lutheran, Anglican, and Calvinist—fared badly at the hands of their own particular groups of non-conformists, whose historical works gradually betray the inherent tendency of Protestantism to rationalism and agnosticism. Probably the only worthy exception in the Protestant field is Johann Lorenz Mosheim, who published his

*Institutiones Historiæ Ecclesiasticæ* in 1726.
But even his volumes contain the sacrosanct Protestant caricature of the Middle Ages and of the
papacy. In fact, from Flacius to Foxe and John
Knox; from Hottinger to Spanheim and Mosheim; from the apostate Sarpi to Voltaire and
his British followers, Hume, Robertson, and
Gibbon; from Hegel to Niebuhr and Ranke;
from James Anthony Froude to Hodgkins and
Coulton; and on to the latest anti-papal scribe of
yesterday, the ancient *Los von Rom* spirit has
seldom slackened in its sturdy vigour. It is true
that in its viler aspects the Magdeburg No-
Popery historian can no longer be certain of a
cultured audience; for the evolution in historical
outlook brought about by the Age of Enlightenment, as the rationalistic period is called, by the
reaction to Voltairianism through the Romanticists, as well as by the rise of the chauvinistic
school of historians, and so on, down to the rise
of modern critical historical science, has been
steady in its tendency to destroy the Protestant
tradition. Through all these changes, historical
Protestantism has fared badly in the house of its
friends. Even the Lutheran Revolt has lost its
old place of honour among them as the standard-
bearer at the gates of modern times. As a religious movement for the betterment of mankind,
even the time-honoured name of Reformation is

being gradually usurped by the phrase Protestant Rebellion.

What is of importance to the Catholic historian during these three centuries of historical development from 1585 to 1885, is that impartial historical scholarship, Catholic and non-Catholic, has marched with constant pace towards the new age of historical enlightenment of our own day. The spirit of critical interpretation, as it becomes more and more refined and freed from the mechanistic view of life and civilization, is bringing out into the light a truer picture of the past of Catholicism. Many names might be mentioned in this respect, but it suffices to recall the place accorded by non-Catholic historians to scholars like LINGARD, JANSSEN, DENIFLE, GASQUET, GRISAR, and VON PASTOR. The historical weapon forged by Luther for a worldwide attack upon the heart of Catholicism, the papacy, has been discovered to be a two-edged sword in the hands of non-Catholic scholars. Anti-Catholic history has been proven to be obscurantist; and the truth is gradually being borne home to the thinking world, as Newman says in his *Essay on Development*—that *to be deep in history is to cease to be a Protestant.*

Humanism, with its secular attitude towards history, broke with the past in the closing years of the fifteenth century. It sheltered for a while the fanatical method of the Centuriators in the sixteenth century, but the Great Awakening of the seventeenth and eighteenth centuries broke with historical Protestantism by examining the very bases upon which that Rebellion had been built. The rationalism of the eighteenth century found its way blocked by the Romanticists, with their avid desire to search out the sources for a fuller and more impartial study of the past, and with the restoration of the medieval times as a most fruitful field for the study of modern institutional life and progress. The fundamental law of the Romantic school—the law of continuity in historical development—was equivalent to an acceptance of the unrivalled position of the Catholic Church in the growth of civilization; and while the spirit of nationalism marred the later productions of the Romantic school, that same spirit led to a movement to which there is no parallel in the historiography of the past: namely, in the publication of source material for the history of the nations. With massive collections of original sources practically pouring from the presses of Europe, the age of slander came to its unworthy end, and the passion for truth rose high in mastery above almost every prejudice. Victor Hugo knew little or nothing of this ultimate development of the struggle he has so graphically sketched between the book made in

stone and the book made of paper; and his prophecy—*Le livre tuera l'Eglise*— can no longer arrest
the fancy.

Into the very heart of this evolution of historical science went from the beginning the best
Catholic scholarship of Europe. The Baronian
cycle of Catholic Church historians includes a
host of workers whose inspiration Baronius was
all through the next three centuries. The immediate influence of the *Annals* was the creation
of a new school of Catholic historiography, devoted rather to the publication of source material
than to the actual narration of Church history;
that would follow in the natural order, after
the sources had been discovered and prepared
critically for publication.

These centuries witnessed a veritable flood-
tide of historical erudition. Into the movement
there came three main streams which have carried
the ecclesiastical historical sciences over all
barriers into the modern critical school of scientific history. The first of these in order of time
is the Jesuit school of historians. The method
accepted by this school was outlined by St.
Ignatius himself in his autobiography, and was
followed by his earliest and greatest biographer,
RIBADENEIRA, and by the Jesuit scholars,
MAFFEI, ORLANDINI and STRADA. The glory of
the Jesuit school is the work of the BOLLANDISTS,

whose three centuries of labors in the field of hagiography (1615–1915) have been so charmingly told in a recent volume by Père DELEHAYE. Even Fueter, who begrudges praise to Catholic historical scholarship in his *History of Modern Historiography,* admits that the *Acta Sanctorum* of the Bollandists inaugurated modern scientific historical study.

The second great movement in the story of modern critical historical scholarship is the creation of the auxiliary sciences of history by the BENEDICTINES OF ST. MAUR. The leader of this school was MABILLON (1632–1707), who founded the science of diplomatic or the critical method of ascertaining the authenticity of documentary material. His work *De Re Diplomatica* (1681) was the standard treatise up to our own day. The basis of the paleographical sciences was laid by another Benedictine, Dom Bernard MONTFAUCON (1655–1741). The science of chronology was reorganized by the Benedictine Dom CLÉMENT in his *L'Art de Vérifier les Dates* (1790). The Benedictines of St. Maur did not confine themselves to the auxiliary sciences, for it was logical that they should apply the methods they taught to the production of volumes of source material. Mabillon's *Annals of the Benedictine Order* have seldom been surpassed for critical scholarship, and the works of D'ACHÉRY,

Bouquet, Durand, and Martène brought to
the science of history an advance which can
scarcely be overestimated. "Before this time
there had either been no attempt to cite sources
or the citations has been hopelessly confused;
there had been no general practice of establishing the genuineness of a text; and there had been
no hesitancy in altering the text of a document to
improve the style. Now documents were search-
ingly examined as to their authenticity, the text
was quoted with exactness, and the citations were
invariably included and given with scrupulous
accuracy." Unfortunately the Benedictines of
St. Maur are still awaiting a Delehaye to
describe their unrivalled place in historiography.

A third group of ecclesiastical historical
studies which were the direct outcome of the
Baronian influence includes collections of sources
in every department of Church history, for the
most part the work of Italian scholars. Only
a few of these really great names need be mentioned: Cardinal Pallavicini, the historian of
the Council of Trent; Archbishop Mansi, the
historian of the Councils; Ughelli, the General
of the Cistercians and the ecclesiastical historian
of Italy; Father Muratori, who found time amid
all his parochial duties to publish 46 volumes
of annals and chronicles for the history of Italy;
the two brothers Ballerini, both priests, who

laid the foundation for critical editions of canon law; and the great Jesuit ZACCHARIA, whose historical works, many of the highest critical value, number 161 in Sommervogel's catalogue.

These scholars gave the impetus to all the notable source collections of the last century. It was the example of their great erudition that aroused such leaders in this field of historical work as Stein and his colaborers in the *Monumenta Germaniae Historica,* Guizot and the work of the *École des Chartes* of Paris, the *Rolls Series* of England, the *Colección de Documentos Ineditos para la Historia de España,* which was completed in 112 volumes between 1842 and 1895, the *Collection de Chroniques Belges Inédites,* in 111 volumes, published in Brussels since 1836, and other smaller but equally important national collections. In the field of ecclesiastical history, mention should be made of the colossal design of Father MIGNE, whose Patrology in 382 volumes outstrips all other enterprises of a similar nature, and also of the various collections of sources for the history of the religious orders, in particular the collections of Dugdale, Helyot, Wadding, Mamachi, Quétif, and the *Monumenta* of the Society of Jesus.

Among those who have made use of these collections of source material for general or partial histories of the Church, and who have achieved fame, are NATALIS ALEXANDER, CLAUDE FLEURY, and probably the greatest Church historian France has produced, TILLEMONT. To these should be added BOSSUET, whose *History of the Variations of the Protestant Churches* is still acknowledged to be one of the impartial histories of the Reformation period.

With the opening of the nineteenth century, ecclesiastical historians were to make use of all the source material published in the previous century, and compendiums of this material began to appear. Among the first of these is the *General History of the Church* (1797) by Signor Pastorini, the pseudonym used by Bishop WALMESLEY, who consecrated John Carroll first Bishop of the United States, at Lulworth, England, in 1790. Another general work, the *History of the Catholic Church*, in five volumes published at Annapolis, in 1829, by Father Charles Constantine PISE, who has the distinction of being the only Catholic priest ever appointed Chaplain to the United States Senate. Manuals of Church history were multiplied with uncommon regularity all through the nineteenth century.

One has but to recall the works of PALMA, WOUTERS, ROHRBACHER, ALZOG, DARRAS, HERGENRÖTHER, DÖLLINGER, JUNGMANN, BRÜCK, GILMARTIN, GUGGENBERGER, KNÖPFLER, FUNK, MARX, and ALBERS, to appreciate this new

trend of Church history writing. These manuals were written in general for the clerical
students of our seminaries and religious novitiates; and while they all suffer from the double
defect of compression and of national outlook,
they have served their purpose in an excellent
manner by bringing within reasonable range the
entire history of the internal and external development of the Church. Nor has there been
any lack of partial histories, that is histories of
the Church in particular countries, such as the
works by HAUCK for Germany, by BRENAN,
LANIGAN, and BELLESHEIM for Ireland, Cardinal MORAN for Australia, FUENTE and GAMS
for Spain, and JOHN GILMARY SHEA for the
United States. In the field of special studies,
particular aspects of Church history have been
treated by DUCHESNE, JANSSEN, DE ROSSI,
DENIFLE, CAUCHIE, GRISAR, and PASTOR, whose
*History of the Popes* ranks as one of the most
learned productions of our day.

The question naturally arises: What has the
Catholic scholarship of the United States accomplished in the field of Church history during the
past century and a half of modern historical
criticism? The volumes of Father Pise stand
alone as the only general history of the Church
written by an American ecclesiastic. If we add
to Father Pise the stately volumes published by

Father REUBEN PARSONS, entitled *Studies in Church History*, and the Manuals of BIRK-HÄUSER, GUGGENBERGER, NICHOLAS WEBER, and the translation of Alzog by PABISCH and BYRNE, there is little to chronicle in the wider field of historical interest. And yet in no land has the Catholic Church ever needed more intelligent and more constant defence against historians whose treatment of the Catholic past is so generously coloured with a pragmatic view of the relations between Church and State. Prescott, Bancroft, Motley, Henry Charles Lea, and especially Parkman, have preëmpted the field of American historiography. They have given to our generation its views of the Church history of the nations they describe, and while it is generally agreed that a revaluation of their sources is needed, no Catholic historian has risen to mastery in this general field. JAMES J. WALSH has probably accomplished more than any living American, as much by the spoken word as by his volumes, to effect a more objective estimate among our non-Catholic compatriots upon the historical past of Catholicism. CARLTON J. H. HAYES has changed decidedly the current of American teaching in his *Political and Social History of Modern Europe*. Thomas J. SHAHAN has written two volumes on the *Beginnings of Christianity* and the *Middle Ages* which are examples of the school of Duchesne and Stubbs. Recently, DE ROO, at a time in life when most men, and especially ecclesiastics, feel they have earned the right to complete rest and reminiscence, has published five volumes of *Materials for a History of Pope Alexander VI,* which have yet to be fully weighed in the balance of modern criticism. Of works in more particular fields, such as ecclesiastical biography, and corporative and institutional history, much has been done that is creditable. But all this class of work—with the exception of such studies as ENGELHARDT'S *Franciscans,* BURNS' *Catholic Schools,* HUGHES' *Jesuits,* CAMPBELL'S *Jesuits,* O'DANIEL'S *Fenwick,* O'BRIEN'S *Hidden Phase* and McCARTHY'S, *History of the United States for Catholic Schools*—is of a minor nature or of limited interest.

The truth is that the future historian of general ecclesiastical history in the United States will find very little worthy of his subject written up to the present. Ecclesiastical history as a science distinct from the *Characterbildung* of the aspirants to the Catholic ministry, has not yet risen above the level of mediocrity in our country. The teaching of Church history in Catholic colleges, seminaries and religious novitiates is below the standards of the already much-confused methods in use in non-sectarian schools, and is mostly confined to the half-hearted memorizing of a textbook whose author or compiler has little precise knowledge of those peculiar apologetic problems in history which constitute our inheritance from Great Britain. Special training for teachers of history in American higher schools is hardly more than a generation old. Special training for teachers of Church history in our religious houses and seminaries has only just begun. The formation of the AMERICAN CATHOLIC HISTORICAL ASSOCIATION (1919) gives promise of creating a national interest in general Church history, but it will be many years before the historical barrier between the Catholic Church and the non-Catholic Christian groups has been leveled by impartial Catholic scholarship.

The continuity between the earliest No-Popery spirit of Great Britain and the present attitude of millions of our countrymen has never been broken. Fear and hatred of Rome have marched side by side with the movement towards the ever-vanishing frontier of the West, which spells all American history in a word. That spirit saw its gravest crisis in the East until almost our own day; but its vigorous persistence beyond the older frontiers must give pause to Catholic scholars who are cognizant of the progress of historical criticism in intellectual centres along the Atlantic Coast.

From the days when the *Simple Cobbler of*

*Aggawam in America* was being read with avidity in the colonies, on through the whole of the colonial period, as can be verified in such collections as Charles Evans' *American Bibliography,* to the days of the notorious anti-Catholic best sellers, *Maria Monk* and *Rebecca Reid,* to John W. Draper's *History of the Conflict between Religion and Science,* and then on to the works of Henry Charles Lea and the famous *Festschrift* of Cornell University, Andrew D. White's *History of the Warfare of Science and Theology,* the literature of the United States has never been without its stern reminders of the dangers inherent in Popery and the Roman communion to America's political and intellectual liberty.

The story of the Catholic press of the country from 1809 to the present has been that of a gallant, and at times, a losing struggle against the spread of a popular anti-Romanism based upon the historical prejudices of the past. It has often been remarked that the key note of American history is to be found in the study of American Presbyterianism; and of the three main arteries of Protestantism, British Calvinism has never been vague in its attitude to Catholicism. Its chief tenet is found as graphically stated in the works of John Knox and his followers as today, four centuries later, upon the walls of vacant houses in its birthplace in Ireland.

The historical objection to Catholicism has been usually presented in our country from this anti-papal standpoint, whether it be in the repetition of old-time shibboleths, such as the dark and gloomy past of the papacy, the black night of the Middle Ages, the incompatibility of Catholicism with national progress, the immorality of Latin America and especially of its clergy, or the various other strategic viewpoints with which we are familiar. But the mood and tense of millions in our country who are neither students nor readers of history, but solely inheritors of the historical viewpoints of the past, will always be found to be indicative, positive, direct, and sure of its ground, when the oldest of all the Protestant objections to the Catholic Church—*the* objection in fact which was made consecrate by the Magdeburg historians—that of Double Allegiance is brought to the surface. There is a tenacity about this popular historical heresy which seems almost to defy explanation.

It would be uncritical, and indeed, inaccurate to say that American Catholic scholars have accomplished nothing to break down the historical barrier which so effectually separates the two great groups of the Christian Church in this country. We have but to recall, as we can recall in all legitimate pride, how on the morrow of Pope Leo's celebrated *Brief on Historical Studies*, August

18, 1883, there came together in the city of Philadelphia a group of Catholic laymen and priests
who founded the AMERICAN CATHOLIC HISTORI-
CAL SOCIETY, which is now rounding out forty
years of loyal service to Leo's ideal. We
have but to recall the historical services rendered by other organizations, such as the
Catholic historical societies of New York, St.
Paul, Chicago, and St. Louis, and the popular
contributions by the Knights of Columbus through
their COMMITTEE ON RELIGIOUS PREJUDICES and
their HISTORICAL COMMISSION. We have but to
mention the work accomplished by the historical
group at the Catholic University of America,
through its quarterly, the *Catholic Historical Review,* or again of popular semi-historical productions such as the *Catholic Builders of the Nation.*
We have to chronicle above all else done to dispel
prejudice and to awaken love for the past of Catholicism that unique accomplishment, the sixteen
volumes of the CATHOLIC ENCYCLOPEDIA. This
helps us to realize that American Catholics have
not been wholly idle. But even with this library
of historical works before us, the truth is that
what has been done is comparatively small in relation to our numbers, our wealth, and our scholarship. What remains to be done is beyond the
listing. And in what remains to be done, both
laymen and priests must have an equal share.

When our Church is ready to place side by side scholars of renown in the historical sciences of equal merit with laymen like STOLBERG, CHATEAUBRIAND, DE ROSSI, MONTALEMBERT, OZANAM, and VON PASTOR, and with priests like LINGARD, NEWMAN, J. A. MÖHLER, JANSSEN, JOHN MORRIS, DE SMEDT, GRISAR, GASQUET, and others, then can we begin to feel that the mission of the Catholic historian has been accepted by our Church.

We need treatises on the classical objections against Catholicism, treatises for the learned as well as for the unlearned.

We need studies of the three main streams of Protestantism in the United States,—Anglicanism, Lutheranism, and Calvinism.

We need Catholic studies in that intricate and difficult subject of the relations between Church and State.

There is wanted a frank and fearless treatise on the historical past, present and future of religious toleration, as viewed in the light of Catholic theology.

Every one of the numerous auxiliary sciences of history is awaiting a Catholic hand to gather up the splendid work accomplished in these sciences by non-Catholic scholars, in order that a common ground may be found for a mutual search for truth.

No book in English on historical method for aspiring Catholic historians, written with all the wealth of Scholastic criteriology, exists; and in the fascinating search for the laws which seem to have dominated human progress in the past, we have abandoned the field to the materialist, the economist, and the non-Christian sociologist.

Even in the most important aspect of historical science, namely, its philosophy, we have allowed the term to become a by-word among those who are willing to follow any logic except that which leads to a belief in divine providence guiding the affairs of men.

Our people could point to no parish in the land where a congregation has enjoyed seven years of historical instruction such as St. Philip Neri insisted should be given week after week by Baronius in Rome, four centuries ago.

The New History found Catholic historical scholarship in America at its lowest ebb fifty years ago. One name is worthy of mention as an exception—that of JOHN GILMARY SHEA. The ever-increasing litany of its successes in the search of historical truth, a search carried on latterly with honor and impartiality in the halls of Harvard, Yale, Cornell, Johns Hopkins, Berkeley, Chicago, and Pennsylvania, as well as in the ranks of the American Historical Association during the past forty years, has not aroused concomitant eagerness on the part of American Catholic scholars, either to profit by the labours of these splendid teachers who devote themselves, in so many cases, to the historical past of the Catholic Church, or to imitate their work in our own colleges and universities.

Of the value of the apparatus for Church-history teaching in our seminaries, little can be said by way of consolation. Ecclesiastical history as the *ancilla* in the house of theology has led a Cinderella-like life, with no princely scholar to raise her from her drudgery and isolation.

Few Catholic laymen of wealth have vision in this respect, for one will look in vain through Catholic libraries to find through their donations complete collections of all the source-material published in the field of Church history since the days of Baronius.

Few of our priests, well prepared as many of them are by their theological studies to enter into the research and critical analysis of the past, are devoting themselves to the task of bringing the knowledge of that glorious past to our people.

The well-known phrase of Cicero—*Nescire quod antequam natus sis acciderit, id est semper esse puerum,* applies with more force to the American priesthood than to any other. On all sides the intellectual decomposition of religious Protestantism is turning the Christian world back to its original division—Nazarenes and pagans. Everything in life has been touched or tainted by this neopagan retrogression, the inevitable result of the cleavage in the sixteenth century.

In the presence of our modern religious indifferentism, deism or latitudinarianism, the leaders of the Christian army of God in the United States cannot keep silent.

The age-old doctrines of the Catholic faith need to be held out to those who have lost all belief or whose belief is crumbling under the rains of constant attack from agnostic thinkers.

There should be going out in a constant stream from the pens of our priests, treatises, books and monographs reasserting with all the wealth and strength of the modern critical historical method the supreme place of the Catholic faith in preserving for the future as it has ever preserved in the past the political security of the nation.

The pages of the Catholic life need to be opened anew to men of good will, that they may see written therein the truth that Christianity and civilization go hand in hand, that social culture and social progress are unthinkable apart from the doctrines of Christ, that all intellectual advancement which breaks with Christian theology is doomed to lead to moral obliquity of vision, that the religious aspirations of the individual as well as of the nation can never be fully developed outside the warmth and glow of Catholic devotional life, and that, beyond all these, in the fearsome uncertainty which hangs over the world, no durable peace is possible unless it be hedged about by the international authority of the Prince of Peace, the Vicar of Jesus Christ on earth.

This is indeed the Age of History, our special heritage from the nineteenth century. If we are to have an explanation of world-history we must first have the true theory, the true *rationale,* the true idea of the true Christian Church and her life through the centuries. Church history is the master-key to open a hundred closed doors. This is what is meant by the phrase *Kirchengeschichte als Weltgeschichte,* the world-record made intelligible by the church-record. Without a knowledge of Church history "we are compelled on matters the gravest, on a field the widest, on subjects of the most fascinating interest, on issues incomparable, to remain in irremediable darkness."

For no other group in the Church of God should the study of Church history have so sacred and so affectionate an appeal as for the clergy. The history of the Church is for the priest not alone the essential and abundant source of all the ecclesiastical sciences, the mistress indeed upon whom ever falls the duty of transmitting all that past centuries have gathered into the fold of

Christ, but also a treasury of *nova et vetera* for the completion of Christ's conquest of the world. As the minister of the Church, the priest is the guardian and the defender of her history. It is to him above all, it is to his intelligence and to his devotion, that the Spouse of Jesus Christ has been confided, with all her annals, her titles to fame, her triumphs over evil, her laws of sanctification, her combats for truth, her victories for Almighty God.

The history of the Church is the history of the priesthood and of the priesthood's holy ministry for souls. All that the Church has ever done, she has done by means of the Christian priesthood—the preaching of the Gospel to the nations, the emancipation of Europe from barbarian rule, the spread of public and private law, the legislation which has kept civilization intact up to modern times, the gradual abolition of slavery, the preservation and transmission of ancient literary culture, the renaissance of art, science, music, and letters—these are the works of the Church, works carried on amid incessant attacks by the forces of evil; and these works the Church has been able to accomplish through her pontiffs, her bishops, and her priests, and in which her priesthood has been the torchbearer of light amid the ever encircling gloom of a paganism that never expires.

*Le livre tuera l'Eglise*—with what surety was it said, with what sureness could it still be said, as one looks back upon the last four hundred years of the *certamen utriusque,* if there were not on the pages of the chronicle the story of a devotion to historical truth which does honour to non-Catholic as well as to Catholic historical scholarship.

The history of the Church has been called one whirling adventure, with the heavenly chariot flying thundering through the ages, the dull heresies sprawling and prostrate, the wild truth reeling but erect.   Each step in advance away from the slanderous age of the *Centuries* on towards freedom from old-time bitterness and iconoclasm has marked a succession of revelations in which the beauty of the ancient Church has become more and more apparent.

Guelphs and Ghibellines are not yet reconciled; but may we not hope that in the warmth and devotion of this better ideal of historical progress, scholars of all creeds, but especially those of our own faith, will continue to bring to light the manifold blessings the Catholic Church has given to men. *Nihil veritas erubescit nisi solummodo abscondi!*

# CHAPTER VII

### THE LITERATURE OF CHURCH HISTORY

It would be idle to begin this chapter with the obvious disclaimer that no attempt is to be made here at a complete survey of so vast a library as that which would contain all the literature ever published on the subject of Church history. No one scholar nor any group of scholars has ever succeeded in so ambitious a plan; and most probably no attempt will ever be made to compile a Universal Bibliography of Ecclesiastical History. All that shall be done in the concluding pages to this little Introduction will be to indicate to the student the principal "pathfinders" for his researches. One guide of this nature which attempted—and failed—to give a complete series of such indications to the student is Edward Bratke's *Wegweiser zur Quellen- und Litteratur-Kunde der Kirchengeschichte,* published at Gotha in 1890.

A universal bibliography of Church history is as impossible a task both from a physical and a systematic standpoint as a universal bibliography of literature in general. It is a banality to say that a complete bibliography of printed books would be of immense service to the student. Such a work would become unwieldy and so defeat its essential purpose; and it is questionable whether an interminable list of all the works which have come from the presses of the world since the middle of the fifteenth century would promote scientific research and critical scholarship.

In the laborious and painstaking work of "path-finding" in a field of such broad dimensions as historical literature there is gained an indefinable something which makes for keener scholarship. Even were a universal catalogue of works on Church history to be compiled, it would become old by the time it left the press. The student has but to turn to those pages of the Louvain *Revue d'Histoire Ecclésiastique* which are devoted to the bibliography of current Church historical works to realize that no one will ever keep abreast of that tide. During the world war (1914–1918), the Louvain *Revue* was suspended but the work of cataloguing and listing all publications in the field of ecclesiastical history went on, and in 1922 a large volume was published containing these indications. Probably many were lost to sight owing to the confusion the war brought to learned circles and to scientific groups in Europe. A universal catalogue of

works, then, is the Ultima Thule of the student:
it will never be reached.   It is like trying to count
the stars with the naked eyes.

Several enterprises of this nature have been
started.   The first is that of Father Francis Mar-
ucelli, a learned priest of Florence, who died in
1703.   His *Mare Magnum omnium materiarum
sive index universalis alphabeticus quorumcunque
scriptorum cujusque idiomatis, etc. etc.,* was to
have 6000 divisions.   The work is still in manuscript in 111 volumes.   About the same time,
Father Raphael Savonarola, of Padua, began a
universal index, with the title *Orbis Litterarius
universus, exhibens materias et scriptores in omni
scientiarum et artium genere, quocumque idiomate
ab initio rei litterariæ usque ad præsens, etc. etc.*
The work existed in manuscript (40 volumes of
which were prepared before the author's death)
in the library of the Theatine Fathers in Padua,
but it has apparently disappeared.   Another contemporary, Father Drouyn, planned an *Index Universalis* in 300 volumes.

The idea or the ideal of such an index has not
wholly died out.   In 1895, an International Institute for Bibliography was founded at Brussels
for the purpose of creating a great card-index for
reference.   Several special bibliographical lists
have been published by the Institute.   The *Bulletin* of the Institute is of little help to the student

of ecclesiastical history.   The best lists will be
the catalogues of the larger libraries in the world
—the British Museum, the National Library, the
Congressional Library, the Vatican Library, etc.
The student who desires to ascertain the status of
the bibliographical sciences (up to 1903) will find
a summary, somewhat confused, in Langlois'
*Manuel*.

A subdivision of the universal index is therefore a physical necessity.   With a view to over-
coming the difficulty inherent in so colossal an
enterprise, courageous scholars have made arbitrary limits for their catalogues and have published them under the title of a general bibliography.   The best of these—Stein's *Manuel de
Bibliographie Générale* (1898) has not escaped
severe criticism, but it is a valuable guide to the
scholar.   It does not wholly supersede the work
of Leon Vallée—*Bibliographie des Bibliographies*
(1883), nor that of Petzholdt—*Bibliotheca Bibliographica* (1866).   Stein had Petzholdt's celebrated book in mind, since he calls his *Manuel* a
*Bibliotheca Bibliographica Nova*.   Of the seven-
teen divisions of Stein's bulky volume, two are of
special interest to the Church historian—*sciences
religieuses* and *sciences historiques*.   In these two
sections the student will learn quickly the best
works with which to begin his research.   Stein
leads to Langlois, whose *Manuel* of historical

bibliography opens the way to every part of the historical field.

The student who has his science well in hand will search Langlois for a general bibliography of Church history. Those he finds will be— as Langlois warns him in his usual satirical way—inadequate in a large measure. They will give to the student only a further stepping stone over the wall to the field itself. The difficulty is augmented since the student is obliged to procure these *wegweiser* or pathfinder books or lists or, at least, to find them in the nearest library. Apart from the bibliographical lists at the beginning of the best manuals of Church history, such as those by Brück, Kraus, Hergenröther, Knöpfler, Alzog, Funk, Marx, Albers, etc., etc., there are a few ex professo attempts at a compilation of sources and books for ecclesiastical history with which the student should be familiar.

Such indications as will be found in Scannell's *Priest's Studies,* in Hogan's *Clerical Studies,* or in the more pretentious *Bibliothek des Priesters,* by Heimbucher (1904), can be passed over as being too elementary to attract the advanced student of Church history. The ecclesiastical historiography to be found in Knöpfler's article *Kirchengeschichte* in the *Kirchenlexicon* (1890) and in Monsignor Kirsch's article *History* in the *Catholic Encyclopedia* (1910) form an excellent basis

for the general study of the literature of Church
history.   Other lists are as follows: the earliest of value is the select bibliography at the
end of Mabillon's *Traité des Études Monas-
tiques* (1691).   Abbé Blanc, who devoted a hundred pages of his *Introduction* (1896) to *Sources
de l'histoire ecclésiastique,* or what he styles a
*Bibliothèque choisie et raisonnée,* has gathered
into that small compass the best account of historical learning up to his time.   His plan of treatment is excellent and many of the authors
cited are estimated with rare impartiality.   Fish-
er's *Select Bibliography of Ecclesiastical History* (1885) is very inadequate.   It will be found
at the end of the volume *Methods of Teaching
and Studying History,* Vol. XIII of Heath's
Pedagogical Library (1898).   Flick's *Rise of
the Medieval Church* (1909) contains a serviceable though incomplete list of books, and Hurst's
*Literature of Theology* (1896) has a section
reserved to ecclesiastical history.   Stang's *His-
toriographia Ecclesiastica* (1897) is a list of
almost all the ecclesiastical historians with comments on their principal works.   It contains nothing of value to the science of historiography.
Collins gives a confused bibliography in his *Study
of Ecclesiastical History* (1903), but his list can
be recommended to the student who follows a
more systematic division of the subject.   Kihn's

catalogue of Church historical works in his *Encyklopädie und Methodologie der Theologie* (1892) is one of the largest lists in print, but it is now out of date. Dom Besse has added a carefully chosen appendix of *Notes Bibliographiques* to his *Études Ecclésiastiques* (1900), but the part devoted to Church history is the weakest. The pretentious work of Sinipoli di Giunta, *Storia Letteraria della Chiesa,* of which two volumes have appeared (1920–22), need not be consulted. Acquoy's *Handleiding,* which has been already mentioned, is a good guide to the sources (though not to the historical works) of Church history. The references to official written sources, unofficial sources, and to unwritten or monumental sources, are already given. The Rev. Francis S. Betten, S. J., published in 1921 a *Partial Bibliography of Church History,* which deserves to be known to all students. It is a *catalogue raisonné* and supplements all lists in other languages with references to publications in English. Fonck's bibliography in his *Wissenschaftliches Arbeiten,* is specially valuable for its references to periodicals. Benigni's latest edition (1916) of the *Historiæ Ecclesiasticæ Propædeutica* contains a list of the principal Church historians and a practical bibliography on the sources and books for the subject by Catholic and Protestant authors.

There remain three volumes which should be in the possession of every student: Bratke's *Wegweiser*, Nirschl's *Propädeutik,* and De Smedt's *Introductio.* The first of these contains guides to knowledge in general through works of an encyclopedic nature, guides to the auxiliary sciences of Church history, special lists for personages of prominence and for local history, and the subsidiary literature of Church history. Bratke writes from the rather stern viewpoint of the Protestant who disbelieves in the impartiality of the Catholic historian, but his choice of books does not suffer in consequence. Naturally, a volume published in 1890 is already much lessened in value. The latter fact is also true of Nirschl's *Propädeutik,* which appeared in 1888. Nirschl is, however, of permanent worth in that section (practically two-thirds) of his work devoted to the auxiliary sciences of Church history. Here the student will find all necessary references to the auxiliary sciences as well as to the problem of method in general. De Smedt's *Introductio,* published nearly fifty years ago, is in spite of its age the best bibliography on ecclesiastical history that exists. It is elementary in its scope, but the scope is the largest of the three books mentioned here specially. The treatises in the *Introductio* are: 1. on the principles of the art of criticism, which considers the science of criteriology in its application to ecclesiastical history and describes the value and use of documentary materials, the value of oral tradition, of inscriptions, etc., etc.; 2. on the divisions of ecclesiastical history; 3. on the sources of ecclesiastical history, namely, documents in general, hagiographical documents, sources for the history of the papacy, for the history of national and particular churches, for monastic history, and monumental sources; and 4. on the auxiliary sciences of ecclesiastical history, with special reference to the publication of source-material. De Smedt's *Introductio* is a veritable mine of references for the Church historian.

The creation of the *Revue d'Histoire Ecclésiastique* by the historical scholars of Louvain, in April, 1900, has made this year a dividing line in the history of ecclesiastical historical bibliography. Each quarterly issue of the Louvain *Revue* has contained a large bibliographical section devoted to every phase of Church history. Its value does not date from the year of its foundation, for there is always a retrospective indication of the best sources and books in its lists. The student who wishes to construct for himself a general and a special bibliography will do well to follow the systematic divisions to be found in the *Revue*. These divisions are as follows:

I.   AUXILIARY SCIENCES.

   1. *Historical Method* in its application to Church History.
     (a)  General studies;
     (b)  Special studies (Criticism);
     (c)  Characteristics of the historical sciences;
     (d)  Philosophy of history;
     (e)  Historiography.

   2. *Bibliography of Church History.*
     A.  General;
     B.  National;
     C.  Historical Bibliographies;
      (a) Bibliographies of sources:
        (1)  Archival sources;
        (2)  Literary sources;
        (3)  Histories of Literature.
      (b) Retrospective bibliographies — Encyclopedias, Guides, Repertories.
      (c) Bibliographies in periodicals:
        (1)  Auxiliary sciences;
        (2)  Sources;
        (3)  Works (General history);
        (4)  Works (Special history).

   3. *Paleography, Chronology, Diplomatic.*

   4. *Archeology.*

5. *Sigillography, Heraldry, Numismat-ics.*

6. *Geography, Linguistics.*

II. PUBLICATION OF SOURCES AND CRIT-ICISM OF SOURCES.

1. *Monumental sources* (Epigraphic texts, etc.).

2. *Archival sources* and diplomatic criti-cism (by centuries).

3. *Literary Sources.*
   A. Writings on the New Testament.
      1. Generalities;
      2. Gospels;
      3. Acts of the Apostles;
      4. St. Paul and his Epistles;
      5. The Catholic Epistles;
      6. Apocalypse.
   B. Ancient Christian Literature (Greek, Latin, Oriental).
   C. Literary Sources of the Middle Ages (by centuries).
   D. Literary sources of Modern and Contemporary Times (by cen-turies).

III. HISTORICAL WORKS.

1. *Universal History.*

2. *General History* (by epochs and cen-turies).

3. *Special History.*

    A.  History of ecclesiastical institutions:

        1. Church and State;
        2. Ecclesiastical law;
        3. Civil law.

    B.  History of Religions.

        1. Comparative religions;
        2. Philosophy of religions;
        3. History of Dogma;
        4. Biblical theology;
        5. Patristic theology;
        6. Scholastic theology;
        7. History of heresies;
        8. Protestantism;
        9. Greek and Russian Churches;
      10. Modernism;
      11. Reunion of Churches.

    C.  History of Liturgical Worship.

    D.  Lives of the Saints—Asceticism, Mysticism.

    E.  History of ecclesiastical sciences and letters.

    F.  History of ecclesiastical art.

4. *History of particular churches; local Church history.*

5. *History of Religious Orders and Congregations.*

This classic division of an ideal Church history bibliography will enable the student quickly to orientate his researches in the latest literature on his subject. There are, however, certain guides, repertories, or manuals of direction, of which he should be cognizant, since the Louvain *Revue* assumes this knowledge on the part of the research-worker. If the student keeps in mind the practical division of an ideal historical library already given—*repertories, didactic works,* and *periodicals,* the following indications will be helpful; especially since these are given only as hints to a larger literature and therefore will not absolve the student from the work of research.

## I.   REPERTORIES

1. *Methodology.*—All the books of importance on the historical method have been mentioned in these pages. After reading Collins, the student should master the short *Outlines* by Fling, and then proceed to the *Introduction* of Langlois-Seignobos. If unable to read any other language but Latin, his next manual should be the *Propædeutica* of Benigni. If the student knows German or Spanish, he will be able to acquire the principles of the historical method in its latest development in Feder or in Villada. Teggart's *Prolegomena to History* (1916) forms a substantial intro-

duction to *The Processes of History* (1918) by the same author. By referring to the current issues of the Louvain *Revue,* to the Minor Notices and Historical News of the *American Historical Review,* and to the Notes and Comments of the *Catholic Historical Review,* the student should not miss any important article or book on the historical method, the philosophy of history, or historiography.

II. *Bibliography.*—The most serviceable manual of general historical bibliography is that of Langlois. The *Quellenkunde der Weltgeschichte* by Herre-Hofmeister-Stub, is the latest addition to the field, but it is of secondary value to ecclesiastical historical research.

(1) For ancient Church history, lists will be found in the best volumes devoted to that epoch. The student might begin, with canonical permission, with Duchesne (*Histoire Ancienne de l'Eglise,* in 3 vols), or Kidd (*History of the Church to 416 A. D.,* in 3 vols.). The trilogy of Batiffol (*L'Eglise Naissante, La Paix Constantinienne,* and *Le Catholicisme Romain de St. Damase à St. Leon*) contains references to recent source material. Wachsmuth's *Einleitung in das Studium der alten Geschi-*

*chte* (1895), and the *Handbuch der klassischen Altertumswissenschaft* (1898–1912), are for the advanced student.

(2) For the Middle Ages, the best repertories are: Potthast, *Bibliotheca Historica Medii Ævi* (to 1500); Chevalier's stupendous *Repertoire des Sources du Moyen Age;* and the scholarly *Guide to the Study of Medieval History,* by Professor Paetow, of the University of California (1917). Chapter one of this last work contains an exceptionally good list of bibliographical works. Professor Thompson of the University of Chicago has published *Reference Studies in Medieval History,* which has a special value for the Church historian. Hurter's *Nomenclator Litterarius Theologiæ Catholicæ,* in 5 vols., Innsbruck, 1903–1910, is a poorly constructed bibliography, but it contains information not easily obtained elsewhere. The indices are not fully reliable.

(3) National bibliographies all contain sections on ecclesiastical history. Among these the student should see:

(a) For England: Gardiner-Mullinger, *Introduction to the Study of English History* (1894), and Gross, *The Sources and Literature of*

*English History from the earliest times to about 1485* (1900).

(b) For France: Monod, *Bibliographie de l'Histoire de France* (1888); Molinier, *Les Sources de l'Histoire de France;* and Hauser, *Les Sources de l'Histoire de France.*

(c) For Germany: Dahlmann-Waitz, *Quellenkunde der deutschen Geschichte* (1912); Wattenbach, *Deutschlands Geschichtsquellen im Mittelalter* (1904).

(d) For Belgium: Pirenne, *Bibliographie de l'Histoire de Belgique* (1902).

(e) For Spain: Ballester y Castell, *Las Fuentas Narrativas de la Historia de España durante la Edad Media* (1908); Altamira, *La Enseñanza de la Historia* (1895).

(f) For Italy: Calvi, *Biblioteca de Bibliografia storica Italiana* (1903); Balzani, *Chronache italiane* (1900).

(g) For Poland: Finkel, *Bibliografja historyi polskiej* (3 vols. 1891–1906); Estreicher, *Bibliografja polska XIX stulecia,* 4 vols. (1912).

(h) For the United States: Channing-Hart-Turner, *Guide to the Study and Reading of American History* (1912).

(4) Retrospective bibliographies (or encyclopedias, dictionaries etc.) are many in number and varied in choice. The Kroeger-Mudge *Guide to the Study and Use of Reference Books* (1925) will lead the student quickly to these. The *Encyclopedia Britannica,* the *New International Encyclopedia, Le Grand Larousse (in Indice),* Meyer's, *Konversations-Lexicon* and Espasa's *Enciclopedia universal,* for general historical subjects are worth consulting. For Church history the *Catholic Encyclopedia* has taken the place of all previous works of this nature, though supplementary aid can be had through the *Kirchenlexikon* (second edition by Hergenröther and Kaulen, 1903). Moroni's *Dizionario di Erudizione Storico-Ecclesiastica,* in 103 volumes, has six index volumes. A group of French Catholic scholars is creating an *Encyclopédie des Sciences Ecclésiastiques* in five dictionaries: *Dictionnaire de la Bible, Dictionnaire de Théologie Catholique, Dictionnaire d'Archéologie Chrétienne et de Liturgie, Dictionnaire d'Histoire et de*

*Géographie Ecclésiastiques, Dictionnaire de Droit Canonique.* The first of these dictionaries is completed; the others are in course of publication. "When completed," says Paetow, "this will be the largest work of reference on religion in any language. It incorporates the highest achievements of Roman Catholic scholarship in France."

For general historical atlases and for those devoted to Church history, references will be found in Paetow (pp. 18–20). Werner's *Orbis Terrarum Catholicus* (1890), and Streit's volumes—*Katholischer Missionsatlas* (1906) and *Atlas Hierarchicus* (1913) are valuable aids to the Church historian, who should never read Church history without such an atlas open before him.

(5) Periodicals containing bibliographical data are published in every country in Europe and in America. A fairly complete list of these will be found in Paetow (pp. 20–24).

III. *Auxiliary Sciences.* A good classification of the auxiliary sciences of history is published by the Library of Congress (1915). Not all of these are needed, as has already been stated, for Church history. The best treatises on the auxiliary sciences to Church history (Paleography, Diplomatic, Chronology, Historical Geography, Archeology, Sigillography, Heraldry, Numismatics, and Genealogy) will be found in Nirschl's *Propädeutik,* in Paetow's *Guide,* and especially in Feder's *Lehrbuch* (1924), where the latest references are given to all these branches. The Louvain *Revue* will enable the student to follow the more recent developments of all these sciences. Of especial value are the references to those periodicals which treat one or the other of these auxiliary sciences, a complete list of them will be found in Feder, pp. 122–123.

## II. DIDACTIC WORKS

1. *Publication of Sources.* Sources may be divided into three kinds—original (archival), literary (contemporary), and monumental (archeological). This division, however, gives but a faint idea of the manifold kinds of sources that exist. The student should compare the tables of sources given by Vincent and Bernheim with those arranged by Feder, since it will benefit him at the outset to

know in what category his source or
sources may fall before searching to see
if they have been published.   Moreover,
the student should know in a general way
the history and the location of all the
principal libraries, archives, and museums of the world before instituting
his research.   The celebrated year book
*Minerva* contains the best information
on the libraries, archives, and museums
of the world.   Under the words *Archive*
and *Bibliotheken* in the *Realencyclopädie*
will be found good bibliographies, and in
Espasa's *Enciclopedia,* under the word
*Museo,* an abundant list of books on the
museums of the world.   Brom's *Guide
aux Archives du Vatican* (1910) is one
of the most successful of the smaller
guides.   Long bibliographies will be
found in the *Encyclopedia Britannica,* in
the *Dictionnaire d'Archéologie Chrétienne et de Liturgie,* and in the *Catholic
Encyclopedia.*

To attempt any worthy catalogue of
the publications of archival, literary, and
monumental sources is beyond the purpose of this short survey.   The *Traité
des Études Historiques* of Jean Moeller
(1887) contains an abundant series of

references to all source-publications for
Oriental, Grecian, Roman, medieval, and
modern history down to the year of its
appearance. De Smedt's *Introductio*
needs no companion volume for the publication of the source-material of Church
history before the year 1876. Nirschl
gives a list of the more important source-
collections for the papacy, the councils,
the relations of Church and State, concordats, canon law, liturgy, rules of religious orders, the *acta* of the martyrs,
patristic collections, and a list of special
collections for the sources of national
and local Church history. These lists
will bring the student to the year 1888,
and they can be supplemented by Oesterley's well-known *Wegweiser durch die
Literatur der Urkundensammlungen*
(1886), although purely ecclesiastical
collections are excluded from his volumes.
The section of Langlois' manual devoted
to this subject is indispensable for the
beginner. Benigni has a list of source-
collections (pp. 141–146; 154–158), but
the most complete catalogue will be
found in Acquoy's *Handleiding*.

II. *Historical Works.* The *mare magnum* of
Church history both Catholic and non-

Catholic knows no chart for its broad expanse or for its depths. Here the student must be grateful for whatever hints are given to him. And it is a benefit to his scientific training that no such chart exists. He is forced to put out in his tiny craft alone and thus find his own way. A compass is never lacking, however, with its four points—universal and general Church histories, special or institutional Church histories, particular and local Church histories, and corporative Church histories or histories of the religious Orders and Congregations.

1. *Universal and General Church Histories.* These will be found listed in all the manuals or handbooks. Rohrbacher's *Histoire Universelle de l'Eglise Catholique* is the best known universal Church history. Originally (1842–49), it was in 29 vols., but has been added to by other editors since that time. The latest addition to this class of works is Mourret's ten volumes entitled *Histoire Générale de l'Eglise* (1921–24). It has been variously estimated. It is not critical in the best sense of the word and, though containing bibliographical no-

tices in each volume, the work lacks
the skill of Kirsch's edition (1915) of
Hergenröther's *Handbuch der allge-
meinen Kirchengeschichte.* Alzog's *Universal Church History* is a good text-
book for the advanced student. The
*Bibliothèque de l'Enseignement de l'His-
toire Ecclésiastique,* begun in 1897, will
be, when completed, a series of monographs that taken together will make up
a universal history of the Church. The
main divisions number about thirty, and
subjects are being chosen illustrating
the principal topics. About twenty volumes have appeared so far, the best
known being by Paul Allard, Tixeront,
Batiffol, Leclercq, Cabrol, Brehier,
Mollat, Jean Guiraud, and Trésal. The
scope of universal Church history is so
vast that it can never be fully mastered
by a single scholar, but like the co-
operative works of Oncken, Helholt,
Pflugk-Harttung, Berr, and others, it
should be the result of a series of
monographs by leading scholars. Some
general histories of the Church by
Protestant authors are of value to the
Catholic student. A list of these will
be found in Paetow (pp. 44–46), and

in Kirsch's article *History* in the *Catholic Encyclopedia.*

2. *Special Church Histories* are divided into three classes—restricted by time, place, and idea limits. By the time limit is meant works dealing solely with any of the four epochs: ancient, medieval, modern, or contemporary. The place limit usually means the history of the Church in a given nation. The ideological or thematic division opens up a host of subdivisions, all of which emphasize the institutional life of the Church. Usually these are confined to the following subjects: the papacy, the councils, Church and State, worship and discipline, confessors of the Faith, monastic rules, acts of the martyrs and lives of the saints, science and letters, ecclesiastical art, heresies and schisms, history of dogma, etc., etc. The *Notices Bibliographiques* at the head of each of Mourret's volumes contain helps to all three of these subdivisions of special Church history (chronological, geographical, and thematic). The bibliographies at the end of the *Cambridge Medieval History* and the *Cambridge Modern History* are unusually large.

It will help the student in his researches to remember that in a general way to the three great time-divisions of history there correspond three classes of source material. Ancient Church history depends to a large extent upon *monuments,* medieval Church history upon *annals,* and modern Church history upon *archival sources.* Since the largest collection of this last class is in the Vatican Archives, the student will do well to keep the year 1883 in his mind as a *terminus a quo* for the more scientific Church historical study. The Louvain *Revue* and the *Historisches Jahrbuch*, an organ of the Catholic Görres Society, will keep the student abreast of the best publications in the field of special Church history. The systematic divisions of the former will enable him to ascertain quickly and accurately what books and articles have appeared in each subdivision of special Church history.

3. *Particular or Local Church Histories* can be found in the national bibliographies, in national Church histories, and in reviews devoted to the Church history of a nation or a locality. Lists of the periodicals devoted to

Church history will be found in Bratke (pp. 164, 197), in Langlois' manual (pp. 119, 176–179; 402–404), and in Fonck (pp. 193–195: historical and literary reviews; pp. 220–222: theological reviews). Poole's *Index* to periodical literature, the *Reader's Guide*, and similar compilations will prove helpful.

4. *Corporative History* or the history of religious Orders and Congregations has an excellent source book in Heimbucher, *Die Orden und Kongregationen der Katholischen Kirche*. This is one of the most thorough bibliographies in existence; the range of its citations to source-collections and historical works is much wider than the title indicates. Volume sixteen (1914–1919)—the bibliographical section of the Louvain *Revue*—supplements the work of Heimbucher with references to all the literature on the religious Orders and Congregations which has appeared in recent years.

## III. PERIODICALS.

### 1. GENERAL HISTORICAL PERIODICALS.

*American Historical Review* (Washington, D. C.); *English Historical Review* (London);

*Historische Zeitschrift* (Munich); *Revue Historique* (Paris); *Revue de Synthèse Historique* (Paris); *History* (London); *Mitteilungen aus der historischen Litteratur* (Berlin).

## 2. FOR GENERAL CHURCH HISTORY.

*Revue d'Histoire Ecclésiastique* (Louvain); *Historisches Jahrbuch* (Munich); *Revue des Questions Historiques* (Paris); *Catholic Historical Review* (Washington, D. C.).

## 3. FOR SPECIAL ASPECTS OF CHURCH HISTORY.

*Literarischer Handweiser* (Freiburg); *Bulletin de l'Ancienne Littérature et d'Archéologie Chrétienne* (Paris); *Bulletin de Littérature Ecclésiastique* (Toulouse); *Analecta Bollandiana* (Brussels); *Archiv für katholisches Kirchenrecht* (Mainz); *Revue Bénédictine* (Maredsous); *Archivum Franciscanum Historicum* (Florence); *Études Franciscaines* (Paris); *Revue Mabillon* (Paris); *Nederlandsch archief voor Kerkgeschiedenis* ('s Gravenhage); *Archivio Storico Italiano* (Florence); *Revista de Archivos, Bibliotecas y Museos* (Madrid); *Bibliothèque de l'Ecole des Chartes* (Paris); *Le Moyen Age* (Paris); *Revue de l'Histoire de l'Eglise de France* (Paris); *Records* of the American Catholic Historical Society (Phila.); *Historical Records and Studies* of the United States Catholic

Historical Society (New York) ; *St. Louis Catholic Historical Review; Illinois Catholic Historical Review* (Chicago) ; *Acta et Dicta* (St. Paul) ; *Römische Quartalschrift* (Rome).

4. CATHOLIC PERIODICALS containing articles on historical subjects (cf. article *Catholic Periodical Literature,* in the *Catholic Encyclopedia,* Vol. xi, pp. 669–680).

*Dublin Review* (London) ; *Polybiblion* (Paris) ; *The Month* (London) ; *Australian Catholic Record* (Sydney) ; *Études* (Paris) ; *Razon y Fe* (Madrid) ; *Stimmen der Zeit* (Freiburg, i. B. ) ; *Tablet* (London) ; *Catholic World* (New York) ; *American Catholic Quarterly Review* (Philadelphia) ; *Studies* (Dublin) ; *Irish Ecclesiastical Record* (Dublin) ; *Civiltà Cattolica* (Rome) ; *Acta Sanctæ Sedis* (Rome) ; *American Ecclesiastical Review* (Philadelphia) ; *Przeglad Koscielny* (Milwaukee) ; *Przeglad historyczny* (Warsaw) ; *Ciudad de Dios* (Escorial).

Whitman's article, *A Bibliography of Church History* (1918–1920), has been reprinted in the *Catholic Historical Review* (New Series, Vol. ii, pp. 333–359), and an excellent summary of Catholic historical studies will be found in Rev. Dr. P. J. Healy's article, *Recent Activities of Catholic Historians,* reprinted in the same review, for July,

1922.  This latter article will round out the list
of periodicals given above and will enable the
student to ascertain the present status of the publication of source-collections in Church history.
Whitney's *S. P. C. K. Bibliography of Church History* (p. 44), may also prove serviceable to the
beginner.

Even with these slight indications or hints
where to obtain material for his subject, it will
not be long before the student realizes that in
the difficult task of finding sources he must travel
for the most part alone.  The graduate student,
for whom these pages are particularly written,
will have the assistance of his teacher and of the
members of his historical seminar; but the work
to be done must be done by himself.  It would
be a mistake, pedagogically speaking, to offer him
more information than has been given in the
pages above.  *Initium dimidium laboris.*  It will
be in his success or failure as a research worker
that the student will learn whether he has the
ability to take his place in the ranks of historical
scholars.

If the beginner, for whom these pages have
been written, has arrived at their conclusion with
the assurance that in the critical or methodic
study of the historical sciences, all the difficulties
of the historian have disappeared, he is risking
a grave disappointment.  The knowledge of

Church historical literature, the conquest of history's rather involved methods of reaching the truth about the past, or the creation of a scientific spirit of inquiry and of critical judgment—these are but apprentice's equipment.

Historical method is not history. Historical criticism is not history. History, to be history, must be written. And if all the advance that has been made in the last half-century in the accumulation of fresh evidence and the introduction of improved methods of research and of critical analysis leaves the student incapable of writing history in a form or fashion that enhances its literary value, then the progress made by the modern methods must be rated as a loss. In other words, the very science itself may prove embarrassing in the mass of riches it brings to light for the student's benefit. The writing of history will never cease to be a branch of art, and all art needs a mastery of the principles of perspective and a just sense of proportion.

Cardinal Newman writes somewhere in his *Historical Sketches:* "I ask something more than to stumble upon the *disjecta membra* of what ought to be a living whole. I take but a secondary interest in books which chop up a saint into chapters of faith, hope, charity, and the cardinal virtues. They are too scientific to be devotional." In the same way, much that is written today in the field of history is too scientific to be historical. The supreme value of the historical method will be not only its introduction to the analytical and synthetic processes of Church historical science, but also its power to place limitations upon the ambition of the student.

Only to a few is given the gift to write history as it should be written, but to many is given the gift of preparing the way for the universal genius Church history needs. Nothing in the way of research, of source publication, of critical essays on minor or major points of history, is valueless. Even the humble bibliographer contributes to the science valuable aid, in sifting out the material for his more fortunate brothers in the field. Some must be gleaners in the field, others will be reapers. But all will have aided towards the harvest.

Twenty years ago, a keen but kindly critic of Church historical science wrote: "Shall we look for the advent of some ecclesiastical Gibbon, or wait the rise of some twentieth century Fleury or Baronius, who shall give us a Church history cast on a more generous scale? Far be it from us to set any limits to the possibilities of the future. For all that we can see, it may be that some such history may be the eventual outcome of the present process of scientific research and historical investigations. But if there should be some gifted historian already in our midst, we should entreat him to hold his hand, for the time is scarcely ripe for such an undertaking. In the wide and varied field of Church history there is still so much to be done in other directions, in considering the bearing of the new evidence, in revising or reversing the conventional verdicts of some of the great figures of the past, and examining into the causes and the meaning of some of its main movements; and no mortal man could hope to do this for the whole course of history."

For this reason, the best historical work of the past generation has naturally and rightly taken the shape of the history of some special subject or of some particular period, or the biography of a prominent figure in the annals of the Church. All these special studies are a necessary element in our historical literature. All of them beckon the student whose ambition is held in restraint by the knowledge that his work must needs be limited in scope and mastered in every detail, if its transmission into writing for his own and future generations is to attain that lively interest and attraction which will keep it forever human.

FINIS

# INDEX